For My Darlings

Copyright ©2010 by Mary Middleton, Backroads Publishing, LLC

All Rights Reserved. No part of this book may be reproduced or transmitted in any form by any means, electronic, or mechanical including photocopying and recording, or by any information storage or retrieval system, except for use in reviews or as may be expressly permitted by the 1976 Copyright Act or by the publisher. Requests for permission should be made in writing to Backroads Publishing, LLC, 2483 Rockland Ave., Wadmalaw Island, SC 29487.

Backroads Publishing and Mary Middleton are not responsible for errors or misrepresentations of fact in Go Local Charleston., nor are we responsible for any injuries that result from visiting the sites listed herein. We have made every effort to ensure the accuracy of prices, hours, phone numbers, and other facts for the sites located in this guide, but because this information is subject to change, we recommend you call ahead before visitng any site. We, Backroads Publishing and Mary Middleton, shall have neither liability nor responsibility to any person or entity with respect to any loss or damage caused, or alleged to be caused, directly or indirectly by the information contained in this book.

Cover Design by Kendra Haskins Design, LLC.
Photo Credits: Middleton Place page 8.

ISBN-13: 978-0-615-33687-9
ISBN-10: 0-615-33687-6

Printed in the United States of America
2010 Edition, First Printing

Acknowledgments

Go Local Charleston never would have made it to press if it weren't for the support of my amazing husband - Frank, thank you is insufficient. A special thank you to my fifteen puppies - your insatiable appetite for learning and your tireless energy levels keep me on my toes, and make me realize how important it is to always have a trick up my sleve to make each day go smoothly. Thank you Mom and Dad for dragging me all over the place despite my predisposition for car sickness. Even though I was usually asleep by the 35th Street Deli, those car trips will always be memorable. To all my family, friends, children, and strangers who either knew they were helping, or who had no clue, thanks for being my guinea pigs. Thanks to Kirsty and Amy, your industry knowledge has been a tremendous asset. Finally, to my editor Karen Charmaine Blansfield, thank you for the refresher course in grammar as well as all your very helpful suggestions and insight; I expect to see you in Charleston soon!

Questions, comments, kudos? I'd love to hear from you:

Backroads Publishing
2483 Rockland Ave.
Wadmalaw Island, SC 29487
mary@golocalcharleston.com
www.golocalcharleston.com

Table of Contents

Introduction   6

How to Use this Guide   8

History With A Twist   9

Birds, and Fish, and Mammals - Oh My!   31

Activities For All.   43

Greenspaces, Trails, Reserves, and Parks   81

"U" Pick It Farms, Farmer's Markets, & Fresh Local Catch .   119

Watering Holes   133

For the Book Worms   145

Playing Around   153

Appendix: Handy Phone Numbers and Information   161

Appendix: Driving Distances   162

Appendix: Getting Around   163

Appendix: Special Events Calendar   167

Appendix: SC Produce Availability   177

Index By Location   179

Index By Attraction   180

Introduction

Go Local Charleston: The Parent's Guide for Children's Activities in Charleston, SC is not your traditional guide book. While most guide books dedicate only a few pages to children's activities, *Go Local Charleston* is entirely dedicated to traveling with kids. It is rooted in both my experiences of traveling with my family since childhood, as well as how my husband and I have learned to travel with our own kids. Having 5 children didn't slow my parents down; we still traveled to National monuments and Niagara Falls. However, what I really remember are all the camping trips and everyday adventures. From my parents I learned that it is possible to make the ordinary extraordinary. We sought out activities in which local people engaged: visiting parks, libraries, beaches, and hole in the wall venues that the average tourist didn't consider or perhaps just didn't know about.

Now that my husband and I have kids, we follow the same pattern that has defined my traveling life: meet the locals, get all the insider tips, and make ourselves at home. Our children don't prevent us from going places; they compel us to slow down and appreciate the voyage. Instead of being destination-driven, we now incorporate many side trips which make the entire outing extraordinary: when we have a hankering for something sweet for dessert, we head to the farm or farmer's market and get locally grown fruits and meet the people who had a hand in bringing those delicious berries to our table as an alternative to the grocery store. Rather than having take out for lunch after a busy day, we head to a beautiful park to dine beneath the shady oaks and, afterwards, run amuck on the playground. We chose to visit Charleston's many museums on days when we know special kid-friendly events will be taking place. Small adjustments like these in our daily lives help us slow down and appreciate our surroundings, and make the ordinary trip for groceries or dining experience extraordinary.

Since many of Charleston's off the beaten path places are pretty hard to find, like the U-Pick farms, hiking trails, or quiet parks, I thought it would be great to have them all collected in one easy to access spot – *Go Local Charleston*! I wanted to share all these cool activities with visitors, young families who already live here and are looking for new and different things to do, or with grandparents who are anticipating a visit with their grandkids.

In an effort to be technologically advanced (which I must confess has been somewhat of a learning curve), I have included quite the multimedia circus to keep you apprised of new findings. Between a Facebook page, Twitter and a blog accessible from the *Go Local Charleston* web page, you'll read reviews of historic sites, see suggested day adventures, and an updated family-focused calendar of activities.

I hope you enjoy these activities as much as our family does. *Go Local* isn't just a book, it's a way of life! I look forward to seeing you out and about in Charleston!

How To Use This Guide

Planning a vacation can be exciting. Vacation gives everyone something to look forward to, and helps us get through the day to day grind that drives us to needing a vacation in the first place. Planning a vacation with children, however, can be demanding. *Go Local Charleston* will facilitate your countdown to leisure time with this handy quick reference guide to activities. Each feature is accompanied by a symbol that you will find next to each activity in the following pages. A brief description of these features is found below:

On the Fly

This is a quick trip, generally lasting less than two hours. You can slip it in between naps or before another event later in the day. This type of trip requires little, if any, planning. Most likely, you'll be home before the next meal. An "On the Fly" trip is proximate to amenities such as meals and bathrooms.

Pack a Lunch

These activities will take \three3 or more hours, so pack a lunch or stop in for a quick bite at a locally owned restaurant. Bathroom facilities and picnic tables can be found on-site or nearby. "Pack a Lunch" excursions are the perfect occasion for combining several activities into a long morning or long afternoon.

Make a Day of It

Locations on the outskirts of town, or full-day kayak trips and hikes are well worth the trip, but require a bit of planning.

While you have the map out, see what other off the beaten path adventures you can wrap into the drive. It's on these less traditional trips that you will see the real Low Country. As often as possible, I have included directions so you're not stuck looking for "the dirt road just past the old grocery at Nine Mile Fork" (which, by the way doesn't exist anymore). Also, in some instances, the GPS just won't get you to your destination without some local insight.

Affordability

Let's face it, traveling with kids isn't cheap. From the snacks and meals out, to hotels and admission fees, to all the historic sites in Charleston, you are sure to spend a pretty penny each day. With that in mind, free admission is highlighted in each section. Quite often, the youngsters under 4 are admitted free anyway! All destinations in *Go Local Charleston* are worth the visit, and the quick-reference guide for admission prices will help in your daily planning.

    ≤ $11.00

    $12.00 - $18.00

    >$18.00

History With A Twist

Since our humble beginning in 1670 when British explorers landed on our shores, many factors have shaped Charleston's landscape: conflicts with the Native Americans, the struggle for independence, seceding from the union, and Mother Nature, of course. These events have woven an intricate patchwork of pirate tales, plantation gatherings, haunted restaurants, earthquake-battered buildings, and fabled slave rebellions that make exploring Charleston's history irresistible.

Charleston's historic sites have a lot to offer visitors of all ages, and your trip to the Low Country would be incomplete without visiting them. Peninsular Charleston has the highest concentration of historic sites, and most of them are found along a one-mile stretch of Meeting Street known as "Charleston's Museum Mile." The sites highlighted in *Go Local Charleston* are more kid-friendly than many other historic sites and houses in the Low Country, with re-enactors, hands-on experiences, regularly scheduled children's programs, and lots of outdoor adventures. You will spend a good deal of time outdoors strolling in most of the plantations and gardens, as well as walking from museums to places to eat. Wear comfortable shoes, and have sunscreen and bug spray handy.

For a complete list of Historic Houses and Museums, visit www.charlestoncvb.org.

Plantations and Gardens

BOONE HALL PLANTATION

Since 1956, Boone Hall has been open to the public and prides itself at being one of America's oldest working plantations. Peaches, strawberries, and tomatoes dot the fields throughout the year. Visitors can tour former slave cabins, listen to the lilting sound of Gullah storytelling, and meander through the rose garden. U-Pick produce varies seasonally, and the "SC Produce Availability" chart on page 177 will be helpful. Plantation admission entitles visitors to numerous tours, including the ever popular tram tour through the working plantation.

Daily and Ongoing Events:

Plantation Tram Tour, 40 minutes.

Butterfly Pavilion, open April - October.

"Exploring the Gullah Culture" in the Gullah Theatre. Showtimes - usually April - October: Monday - Saturday 11:30 a.m., 1:30 - 3:30 p.m., Sunday 2 – 4 p.m.

Admission: $17.50/Adult, $15/Senior (65+)/Military/AAA members, $7.50/Child (6-12). Children 5 and under are FREE.

Hours: Labor Day through Mar. 8: Mon. – Sat. 9 a.m. – 5 p.m., Sun. 1 p.m. – 4 p.m.; Mar. 9 through Labor Day: Mon. - Sat. 8:30 a.m. – 6:30 p.m., Sun. 1 p.m. – 5 p.m. Closed Thanksgiving Day and Christmas Day.

1235 Long Point Road | Mount Pleasant
(843) 884-4371
www.boonehallplantation.com

CYPRESS GARDENS

Cypress Gardens is a freshwater swamp populated with approximately 80 acres of Bald Cypress and Swamp Tupelo. The trail system around the swamp is 4.5 miles, or you can borrow one of the flat-bottomed boats to tour the swamp and see Bald Eagles, Great Blue Herons, Wood Storks, native and migrating song birds, reptiles, and, of course, alligators. Visit the on-site aquarium and discover what lurks beneath the swamp water. A stroll through the butterfly garden is breathtaking and a must for the youngsters.

Go Local Charleston's
Must See Sites

Ages 2 - 5
Children's Museum of the Lowcountry

Ages 6 - 9
Old Exchange and Provost Dungeon

Ages 10 - 14
Patriots Point Naval and Maritime Museum

Admission: $10/Adult, $9/Senior (65+), $5/Child. Children 5 and under are FREE.

Hours: Daily 9 a.m. - 5 p.m. The last guests are admitted at 4 p.m. Closed Thanksgiving, Christmas Eve, Christmas Day, and New Year's Day.

3030 Cypress Gardens Rd. | Moncks Corner
(843) 553-0515
www.cypressgardens.info

MAGNOLIA PLANTATION AND GARDENS

Kids love strolling (and running) around the circa 1680 gardens of this historic site, though the significance of the Pre-Revolutionary War plantation house might be lost on the youngest kids. They will all enjoy the Zoo and Nature Center, where children can feed the animals by hand.

Admission (Gardens and Grounds): $15/Adult, $10/Child (6-12). Children under 6 are FREE. Additional tours include the house, nature train and boat rides, and the Slavery to Freedom tour at a cost of $7 each per adult and child (6-12). Again, children under 6 are FREE.

Admission (Audubon Swamp): $7/Adult, $7/Child (6-12). Children under 6 are FREE.

Hours: Daily, including all holidays, 9 a.m. – sunset. Last tickets are sold about 5 p.m.

3550 Ashley River Rd. (Hwy. 61) | West Ashley
(843) 571-1266
www.magnoliaplantation.com

MIDDLETON PLACE

Middleton Place is more than a National Historic Landmark. Its sprawling landscaped gardens - the oldest in America - nature walks, tours, kayaking, horseback riding, and stable yard offer hours of education and entertainment. Stay the day and enjoy a picnic under the oaks. Of particular note is Plantation Days, occurring one weekend in October and one weekend in November. Showcasing 18th and 19th century life, re-enactors and hands-on activities fascinate the children.

Daily and Ongoing Events:

Demonstrations in the stable yards by craftspeople and guided tours occur daily.

Admission: $25/Adult, $5/Child (7-15). Children 6 and under are FREE. Guided house tours, carriage tours, horseback riding, and kayak rental have additional fees. Order tickets online and save $5.

Hours: Daily 9 a.m. – 5 p.m. During the summer months you are welcome to wander the grounds until dusk as long as you have entered and paid before 5 p.m.

4300 Ashley River Road (Hwy. 61) | Charleston/Summerville
(843) 556-6020 or (800) 782-3608
www.middletonplace.org

OLD SANTEE CANAL PARK

Though most of America's first summit canal (an artificial waterway that connects two rivers of different height levels through a series of locks which gradually bring the waterways to the same height level) lies beneath the waters of Lake Moultrie, Stony Landing remains as a visible reminder of one of our country's earliest achievements. The summit canal was built to expedite barge travel and trade in the early 1800s. Old Santee Canal Park grounds include the lower portion of the original canal, a plantation house, and beautiful views of the upper Cooper River and Biggin Creek. This is a nice destination for the older children, as the importance of a canal will probably be lost on the youngest visitors.

Admission: $3/Age 7-64, $2/Senior 65+. Children 6 and under are FREE.

Hours: Daily 9 a.m. – 5 p.m.

900 Stony Landing Road | Moncks Corner
(843) 899-5200
www.oldsanteecanalpark.org

Did You Know?

Did you know that in the early days of Charleston the city was often visited by pirates? Pirates that were captured were sent to jail in this dismal prison - can you name this prison?

Find the answer on page 19.

Museums and Educational Adventures

CHILDREN'S MUSEUM OF THE LOW COUNTRY

Slip behind the Visitor's Center on Meeting Street (along Charleston's Museum Mile) and you'll find the Children's Museum. The first hands-on children's museum in the Low Country, Children's Museum of the Low Country (CML) has eight interactive exhibits for children ages 3 – 12. A special toddler room was constructed for children two and under. Exhibits focus on the history of the area in a very kid-friendly way: Water Wise, The Pirate Ship, Children's Garden, and Charleston Market. Creativity Castle, Castle Stories, and the Raceway exhibits spark the imagination while building skills. I can't tell you how many days we've never made it past the golf balls in the Raceway to see the rest of the museum.

Daily and Ongoing Events:

Tuesdays 10:15 a.m. Petit Français - Learn French and explore the French culture (Ages 2 -5).*

Tuesdays 3:30 p.m. Kid Café - Play with your food and discover how to eat well and stay healthy at the same time. FREE.

Wednesdays 11:00 a.m. Botany Buddies - Explore the KidGardens, plant a seed, water it, and watch it grow. FREE.

Wednesdays 3:30 p.m. Drop In and Draw. FREE.

Thursdays 10 a.m. Storybook Scramble - read along and share your favorite stories. FREE.

Thursdays 3:45 p.m. High Five Art! - Art classes (Ages 5 - 12).*

Fridays 10:30 Mini Masters - Art classes.*

*$5/Child with Museum admission. Registration is required.

Admission: $7/Person. Children under 12 months are FREE.

Hours: Closed Mon. Open Tues. - Sat. 9 a.m. – 5 p.m., Sun. 1 – 5 p.m. CML is closed on New Year's Day, Easter, July 4th, Thanksgiving, Christmas Eve, and Christmas Day.

25 Ann St. | Charleston
(843) 853-8962
www.explorecml.org

FORT MOULTRIE
AND FORT SUMTER NATIONAL MONUMENTS

During the Revolutionary War, Fort Moultrie on Sullivan's Island was used to hold back the British invasion. Known for its Palmetto-log fortifications, Fort Moultrie is a landmark on Sullivan's Island beach along the Atlantic Ocean. Through the duration of World War II, as part of the coastal defense of the United States, Fort Moultrie protected Charleston Harbor. As weapons technology became more complex, the need for a fort became unnecessary. The restored fort now walks the visitor back in time from World War II to the first Palmetto-log fortification.

A newly opened exhibit at Fort Moultrie entitled "Sullivan's Island and the Slave Trade" explores Charleston's large role during the slave trade from 1707 through 1799. Examples of shackles and ID badges slaves were made to wear are on display and serve as a reminder to us all never to let such inequities occur again. Ask about the Junior Ranger Program, which is available at both sites. A completed program, checked by a ranger, entitles children aged 12 and under to receive a badge and certificate – a rather nice souvenir.

Another fort in Charleston's line of defense was Fort Sumter. Construction on the fort, located in the mouth of Charleston Harbor, began in 1829. Fort Sumter is a man-made fortification built with material from as far away as Boston, Mass. The pentagonal shaped fort has 5- foot thick walls towering 50 feet above the low tide mark. Fort Sumter was not yet complete when, on Apr 12, 1861, the first shots of the Civil War rang out. After 34 hours of battle Fort Sumter surrendered.

Admission: $3/Adult (16-61), $1/Senior (62+), $5/Family. Children under 16 are FREE.

Hours: Fort Moultrie is accessible by car and is open daily from 9 a.m. - 5 p.m. except for New Year's Day, Thanksgiving Day, and Christmas Day.

Fort Moultrie (a unit of Fort Sumter)
1214 Middle St. | Sullivan's Island
(843) 883.3123
www.nps.gov/fomo

Visitor Education Center and Fort Sumter

Fort Sumter has a seasonal schedule and is only accessible by ferry, which departs from two locations: Liberty Square (next to the South Carolina Aquarium) at 340 Concord St., and Patriots Point Naval & Maritime Museum at 40 Patriots Point Rd., Mt. Pleasant. Visit www.nps.gov/fosu/planyourvisit/hours.htm for detailed hours when traveling by private boat.

Admission: There is no admission fee for those who arrive at Fort Sumter by private boat. Visitors using the ferry should contact SpiritLine Cruises for ticket information and reservations: 1(800) 789-3678 or www.spiritlinecruises.com.

Hours: Daily 8:30 a.m. - 5 p.m. Closed New Year's Day, Thanksgiving Day, and Christmas Day.

Fort Sumter Visitor Education Center at Liberty Square
340 Concord St. | Charleston
www.nps.gov/fosu

GIBBES MUSEUM OF ART

In 1858 the Carolina Art Association was established, and by 1905, the Gibbes Museum of Art opened its doors. The Gibbes is located in the historic district on Charleston's Museum Mile. The collection consists of over 10,000 works of fine art, mostly American artists with a Charleston or Southern connection. Annual special exhibits round out the collection. If you happen to have an internet connection while planning your trip and some time on your hands, the Gibbes' website offers in depth interactive exhibits on-line that will educate and entice the youngest visitors.

There is no public parking at the Gibbes; however, on-street parking is available. The surrounding streets house 2 parking garages for your convenience.

Daily and Ongoing Events:

Junior League of Charleston Community Days*
Saturday, February 20 from 10 a.m. – 1 p.m.
Saturday, April 17 from 10 a.m. – 1 p.m.

Community Day at the Gibbes Museum of Art is filled with free activities including hands-on activities for families, museum tours, and musical performances for all ages.

*As of the publication date. In the past, Community Days have also been held during September and December.

Admission: $9/Adult, $7/Senior, Students and Military, $5/Children (6-12). Children under 6 are FREE.

Hours: Tues. - Sat. 10 a.m. – 5 p.m., Sun. 1– 5 p.m.

135 Meeting St. | Charleston
(843) 722.2706
www.gibbesmuseum.org

Answer to Did You Know page 14.

The Provost Dungeon housed notable pirates like Stede Bonnet, along with those the British deemed as less law abiding citizens. Thomas Heyward, Jr. and Arthur Middleton are among the unfortunate Charleston residents incarcerated in the Dungeon. The Provost Dungeon was constructed in the late 1700s and is open for tours daily.

OLD EXCHANGE AND PROVOST DUNGEON

When two British sailing sloops made their way up the Ashley River in 1620, they landed in what they would call "Charles Town." Quickly, Charles Town grew, and the need for goods and materials increased. Broad Street was the center of the waterfront community and the main intersection of thoroughfares for maritime traffic, so if the town were to survive, a trading port needed to be established near Broad Street. By 1772 the Exchange was constructed. Since that time, the history of the Exchange has been rich with stories of pirates, wars, and a tea party.

Beneath this formidable building lies the Provost Dungeon. Its name leaves little to the imagination, and upon entering, you'll immediately be grateful for your place in history as well as your ability to abide by the law. Without any means of heating and no dehumidifiers, many prisoners fell ill and met their demise.

Today, the Old Exchange and Provost Dungeon remains a cornerstone of the historic district. Draped in flags and flanked by re-enactors (which Charleston has no shortage of), visitors can step back in time while exploring the artifacts and wandering the halls of the Exchange and its dungeon. Have a picnic lunch or stroll through Waterfront Park behind the Exchange.

Admission: $7/Adult, $3.50/Child (7-12). Children 6 and under are FREE.

Hours: Mon. - Sun. 9 a.m. – 5 p.m.

122 East Bay St. | Charleston
(843) 727-2165
www.oldexchange.com

PATRIOTS POINT NAVAL AND MARITIME MUSEUM

In 1975 the USS Yorktown arrived in Ch... the first ship in the collection of the Naval & Maritime Museu... Since that fateful date, Patriots Point has become a port for military aircraft, destroyers, submarines, a Coast Guard cutter, and more military equipment from WWII to the present. Also on site are a replica base camp from the Vietnam era that tells the story of life on land during the conflict as well as the Congressional Medal of Honor Museum, which offers interactive exhibits highlighting the bravery and sacrifice of our armed forces.

Admission: $16/Adult, $13/Senior and military with ID, $8/Child (6-11).

Hours: Daily 9 a.m. – 6 p.m.

40 Patriots Point Rd. | Mt. Pleasant
(843) 884.2727
www.patriotspoint.org

POWDER MAGAZINE

Located just off Meeting Street on Charleston's Museum Mile, the Powder Magazine is the oldest public building in North and South Carolina. This unassuming brick building has 3-foot thick walls and four groin arches. Why would a building be so fortified, you might wonder? Well, in past lives, the building protected wine, horses, and printing presses, but the original purpose of the Powder Magazine was storing gun powder. Should an accidental explosion or enemy invasion occur, these strong walls and groins were designed to implode, protecting the neighbors.

Restored to its original appearance, the Powder Magazine is now an educational museum with frequent living history presentations. Not a very hands-on museum, it caters to older children and adults; each weekend - sometimes Fridays and sometimes Saturdays, depending on the artists - interpreters and local craftspeople depict various periods to showcase the art and trade of that particular period. Programs last from 12 – 4 p.m. and are included in the admission. The Powder Magazine is not large, so events are standing room only. No reservations are required.

Admission: $2/Adult, $1/Student, $5/Family.

Hours: Mon. - Sat. 10 a.m. – 4 p.m., Sun. 1 – 4 p.m.

79 Cumberland St. | Charleston
(843) 722-9350
www.powdermag.org

THE CHARLESTON MUSEUM

Founded in 1773, the Charleston Museum is America's oldest museum and part of Charleston's Museum Mile. Its extensive and diverse collection becomes clear as you wind through the halls, moving in and out of centuries of Charleston history. Upon entering the main hall, most children and adults alike are immediately drawn to the Atlantic Right Whale skeleton hanging from the ceiling. Many children, never having seen a whale skeleton, call it a dinosaur, as their familiarity with skeletons is usually with the T-Rex or Brontosaurus in science museums. Other highlights include the newest addition to the museum, "KidStory," a hands on kid-centric exhibit. Of course, no visit to the Museum is complete without seeing the polar bear and mummy! Kid tours are available throughout the week, as are scavenger hunts, special weekend programs and hands-on children's classes.

Daily and Ongoing Events:

Toddler Days:
Toddlers (18 months – 3 years) and a grownup friend can play and explore in the Museum, play in the classroom doing crafts and finger paint, or play in the puppet theater or sandbox. The program is offered every other Wednesday from 10 – 11 a.m. Price includes Museum admission and program for one child and one adult. $6/Member; $9/Non-member. Reservations are required.

Kid Tours:
First Wed of each month and every Wed in Jun and Jul, Kid Tours highlight artifacts from the Museum collection that have fascinated children for generations, like the Egyptian mummy. Tours begin at 3:30 p.m. and include a craft or activity. $10/Adult, $5/Child. Children under 3 and Museum members are FREE. Reservations are not required.

Family Fun Events:
Every month (usually the 2nd Sat), the Charleston Museum offers a special Sat program dedicated to providing an educational and exciting experience for the whole family. From Country Fair days to Archaeological Extravaganza digs, families meet scientists, historians and craftspeople, and have fun with hands-on projects, all of which are included in Museum admission. $10/Adult, $5/Child. Children under 3 are FREE. Reservations are not required.

Home School History Days:
The 2nd Tuesday of every month, from September – May, the Museum welcomes homeschoolers to participate in a special day of theme-based hands-on learning. Reservations are recommended but not required. FREE for members and FREE with general admission to the museum.

Admission: $10/Adult, $5/Child (3-12). Children 2 and under are FREE.

Hours: Mon. - Sat. 9 a.m. – 5 p.m., Sun. 1 p.m. – 5 p.m. Closed New Year's Day, Easter Day, Thanksgiving Day, Christmas Eve afternoon, and Christmas Day.

360 Meeting St. | Charleston
(843) 722.2996
www.charlestonmuseum.org

THE NORTH CHARLESTON & AMERICAN LAFRANCE FIRE MUSEUM AND EDUCATIONAL CENTER

I still can't put my finger on what it is about fire trucks, sirens, and lights that attract children so much. Our own daughter gets so excited whenever we see the "siren trucks" as she calls them. I guess I'd rather the sirens and lights be exciting than the flames generally associated with them! If your children are like the kids I know, the Fire Museum will be a huge hit. Located next to the Tanger Outlet Mall in North Charleston, the Fire Museum is filled with hands-on experiences that will educate and entertain children and adults alike. It houses the biggest collection of restored LaFrance apparatus in the country – 18 vehicles ranging in age from 1886 to 1969.

Parents will appreciate the learning experience and can take home lessons and fire escape plans that are sure to protect your family for years to come. Kids will love the trucks, the equipment, and the hands-on - and very realistic (brand new from American LaFrance, Co.) - fire truck cab with all the bells and whistles of present-day engines. Turn on the engine and feel the seats bump up and down as the simulation screen on the windshield shows the truck weaving through traffic. The horn even works, and is rather loud.

Admission: $6/Age 13+. Children under 13 are FREE with paying adult.

Hours: Mon. - Sat. 10 a.m. – 5 p.m., Sun. 1 – 5 p.m.

4975 Centre Pointe Dr. | North Charleston
(843) 740-5551
www.legacyofheroes.org

Walking Tours

You can't visit an old city without thoughts of ghosts roaming the streets. As night falls in Charleston, the ghost tours come alive. Hear about some of our most famous pirates, visit haunted graveyards, learn about buried treasure, and, if you are lucky, see a lingering spirit or two. These tours are definitely for the older kids because they can be pretty spooky.

BULL DOG TOURS

"Charleston Ghost and Dungeon Tour"

Explore back alleyways, churches, and cemeteries while listening to sometimes funny and sometimes creepy haunted Charleston lore. Each tour lasts 90 minutes.

Admission: $18/Adult, $10/Child (7-12).

Hours: Mar. 1 - Nov. 30 Tues. - Sat. 7 p.m., 9 p.m.

"Haunted Jail Tour"

Go behind the scenes of the Old City Jail, temporary home to some of Charleston's famous criminals, war prisoners, and pirates, including Stede Bonnet and Issac Hayne. Some of the original cells and warden's quarters are still intact, despite being over 200 years old. This tour is 45 minutes long.

Admission: $18/Adult, $10/Child (7 – 12).

Hours: Nightly 7 p.m., 8 p.m., 9 p.m., 10 p.m. Please call for availability. Times are subject to change.

40 North Market St. (Rainbow Market) | Charleston
(843) 722-TOUR
www.bulldogtours.com

OLD CHARLESTON TOURS

"Ghost Tour"

Mike Brown, an internationally acclaimed guide featured on the BBC, SCETV, and the Home and Garden Channels, will lead your Ghost Tour through graveyards, alleyways, and other spooky sites around town. The tour lasts 90 minutes. Departs from Washington Square Park.

Admission: $18.50/Adult, $10.50/Child. Reservations are required. Save $3 by purchasing tickets online!

Hours: 7:30 p.m., 9:30 p.m.

"Pirate & Dungeon Tour"

Mike Brown's Old Charleston Pirate & Dungeon Tour highlights buried treasure, pirates, ship battles, and sword fights, ending with a tour of the Old Exchange and Provost Dungeon — at night! Creepy! This tour lasts two hours. Departs from Washington Square Park.

Admission: $22.50/Adult, $14.50/Child. Reservations are required. Save $3 by purchasing tickets online!

Hours: 1:30 p.m.

Washington Square Park on Broad St. | Charleston
(843) 568-0473
http://www.oldcharlestontours.com/ghosttour.html

TOUR CHARLESTON

Tour Charleston tours have been featured on CNN, MSNBC, The Discovery Channel, The History Channel, and Home and Garden TV (HGTV), as well as in Wall Street Journal, Southern Living Magazine, USA Today, and Travel & Leisure Magazine and the Home and Abroad travel-planning company. Julian T. Buxton, III, the well known author of The Ghosts of Charleston and founder of Tour Charleston, is the Charleston Expert for Home and Abroad. When you embark upon "The Ghosts of Charleston Tour," you will visit the Unitarian Church Graveyard – one of the most famous in the city and only accessible for a tour with Tour Charleston! Mr. Buxton recommends his tours for children over 7 years old, as the content is not appropriate for younger visitors – either they don't understand the concepts, or the ideas of ghosts can be a bit scary.

"The Ghosts of Charleston"

Wander the streets of the Charleston under the cover of darkness, listening to tales of famous ghosts as well as of haunted Bed and Breakfasts and houses, and learn more about the deeply rooted superstitions of Charleston's Gullah culture. Tours depart from the Circular Fountain at Waterfront Park off East Bay Street. Use activity code #602 when speaking to the operator to make reservations for this tour.

Admission: $18/Adult, $12/Child. Tours often sell out, so call ahead to make reservations.

Hours: Mon. – Sun. 5 p.m., 7:30 p.m., 9:30 p.m. Please arrive 15 mins. prior to tour.

"The Ghosts of Charleston II"

This ghost tour will give you all the spook of the original "Ghosts of Charleston" tour, only you will explore the secrets of Charleston on the edge of the city limits. Tours depart from the fountain on the corner of King St. and Calhoun St. on Marion Square. Use activity code #696 when making reservations for this tour.

Admission: $18/Adult, $12/Child. Tours often sell out, so call ahead to make reservations.

Hours: Mon. – Sun. 7 p.m., 9 p.m. Please arrive 15 mins. prior to tour.

"The Pirates of Charleston"

Listen as experienced tour guides recount stories of pirates Stede Bonnet and Anne Bonny while you walk the Charleston streets. Imagine yourself a city resident during the time of Blackbeard the pirate and envision the battles taking place from the 1650s to 1720s, also known as the "Golden Age of Piracy." Tours depart from the Circular Fountain at Waterfront Park off East Bay Street. Use activity code #607 when speaking to the operator to make reservations for this tour.

Admission: $18/Adult, $12/Child. Tours often sell out, so call ahead to make reservations.

Hours: Mon. – Sat. 10 a.m., 4 p.m. Please arrive 15 mins. prior to tour.

(843) 723-1670 or (800) 854-1670
Reservations with Zserve (800) 979-3370
www.tourcharleston.com

BIRDS, AND FISH, AND MAMMALS - OH MY!

From a walk through Charles Towne Landing's Animal Forest to learn about the Low Country's resident and former resident animals, to the South Carolina Aquarium Mountain to Sea exhibits, our birds, fish, and mammals (and reptiles and amphibians) have much to teach you. Children will learn how their daily lives impact the natural world. They will observe that it is possible to rescue and rehabilitate injured animals. Many hands-on opportunities are available, allowing the kids, and interested adults, to hold snakes, turtles, lizards, or any other willing creature.

And, all learning opportunities aside, whenever we are feeling a bit out of sorts, a visit to an animal park or the aquarium will always bring smiles to our faces.

BEE CITY HONEY BEE FARM AND PETTING ZOO

Never thought a whole city would be voluntarily given over to the bees, did you? Yet, Bee City is all that and more. Not only do you get to learn about a very important, though sometimes painful, member of the food chain, you get to hand feed a slew of animals, including lemurs and deer as well! Bee City is a popular field trip destination for school children; however, on Fridays and Saturdays, individuals can take part in the fun as well. If you have a group of 15 or more, you can schedule a visit for other days of the week. I've listed all hours of operation, should you have the opportunity to get a group together.

Upon arrival, you will learn about the equipment used during collection, see a hive through a glass observation box, and check out the tasty local honey treats. The Petting Zoo is also buzzing with activity: deer, monkeys, lemurs, wallabies, alpacas, llamas, and serval cats. And a day couldn't go by without the Low Country's assortment of snakes, lizards, turtles, and frogs, all found in Bee City's Nature Center.

Since you'll have spent a good portion of your day at Bee City, you will be happy to know there is a Bee City Café with some pretty good food. But if you're like us and just can't pass up the opportunity for a picnic, there are outdoor tables as well.

Admission: $4/Ages 3+. Children under 3 are FREE. Field trips require reservations, which range from $4 - $12/Person. Variations in price relate to the number of additional activities you wish to include in your visit. For example, an educational program on honey bees, bottling honey, making a beeswax figurine, rolling honeycomb candles, and touring the petting zoo and nature center are not all included in the basic admission fee of $4.

Hours: Sept. – May Fri., Sat. 9 a.m. – 6 p.m.; Jun,. Jul., Aug. Tues., Wed., Thurs. 9 a.m. – 5 p.m., Fri., Sat. 9 a.m. – 6 p.m.

Directions: From downtown Charleston, take I-26 to Exit 199-A. Take Hwy. 17-A South to Hwy. 61 North. Approximately 9 miles later, you'll cross the Edisto River Bridge. Just 3 miles past the bridge, turn right onto Bittersweet Lane. Follow the signs from there to Bee City. Since Bee City is quite close to Givhens Ferry, you might consider rounding out the day with another trip to this park. (See Greenspaces, Trails, Reserves, and Parks page 92).

Go Local Charleston's
Must See Sites

Ages 2 - 5
Charles Towne Landing

Ages 6 - 9
Caw Caw Interpretive
Center

Ages 10 - 14
Center for Birds of Prey

1066 Holly Ridge Ln. | Cottageville
(843) 835-5912
www.beecity.net

CAW CAW INTERPRETIVE CENTER

Another winning cultural and natural history site from Charleston County Parks and Recreation, Caw Caw was once part of a rice plantation; now it is host to songbirds, otters, deer, alligators, swallow-tailed Kites, and bald eagles. Meander through six miles of interpretive trails over elevated boardwalks through the wetlands and swamp. Dogs and bikes are not permitted.

Daily and Ongoing Events:

Regular programs include bird walks, interpretive walks, reptile programs, edible and medicinal plant talks and walks, and slide presentations.

Admission: $1/Person. Children 2 and under are FREE.

Hours: Wed. – Sun. 9 a.m. – 5 p.m. Closed Mon. and Tues.

5200 Savannah Hwy. | Ravenel
(843) 889-8898 or (843) 795-4368
www.ccprc.com/index.aspx?nid=53

CENTER FOR BIRDS OF PREY (CBOP)

The mission of the CBOP is "to identify and address vital environmental issues through avian medicine, educational, research and conservation initiatives" (www.thecenterforbirdsofprey.org). Working alongside Avian Conservation Center, US Fish and Wildlife, and SC Dept. of Natural Resources, the Center provides a haven for injured birds as well as educational opportunities for all ages. Over 30 species of birds of prey reside at the Center.

Did You Know?

Did you know that bison once roamed freely around Charleston? In fact, bison weren't the only large mammals that once called the Low Country home. Can you guess what other wooly beast left us a clue?

Find the answer on page 36.

Daily and Ongoing Events:

Daily activities — weather permitting, as the Center is primarily outdoors — include guided walking tours at 10:30 a.m. and 2 p.m. and flight demonstrations at 11 a.m. and 3 p.m.

Admission: $12/Adult, $10/Youth (6 -18). Children under 6 are FREE (but must be accompanied by parent or guardian).

Hours: Thurs. – Sat. 10 a.m. – 5 p.m. Closed Sun. – Wed. Closed Thanksgiving, Christmas, and New Year's Day.

Directions: From downtown Charleston take Hwy. 17 North through Mt. Pleasant to Awendaw, approximately 15 miles. Turn right on Sewee Rd. At the entrance gate, turn right into the Center.

872 Sewee Rd. | Awendaw
(843) 971-7474
www.thecenterforbirdsofprey.org

CHARLES TOWNE LANDING STATE PARK

In 1670, English settlers landed in what was to become the birthplace of the Carolinas colony. In 1970, Charles Towne Landing, listed on the National Register, was opened to the public. It houses 664 acres of marsh-front park, a natural habitat zoo (including bison and elk!), interpretive trails, and the original settlement area. Guided tours and special programs are available, but many require advance registration. Call ahead or check the website for schedule, reservations and fees.

Daily and Ongoing Events:

1st Saturday: 17th Century Musket Demonstrations.
2nd Saturday: Event Reflecting Monthly Theme*.
3rd Saturday: Cannon Firing (except January and August).
4th Saturday: Crafts for Kids.

*In the past, themed family programs ranged from "A Day in the Life of a Colonist," to "From Seeds to Shillings: Gardens and Agriculture," to "Ceremonies of the Cultures."

Public programs are also held Wednesday – Saturday and vary daily.

Admission: $5/Adult, $3.25/SC Senior, $3/Child (6-15). Children 5 and under are FREE.

Hours: Daily 9 a.m. – 5 p.m. Closed Christmas Eve and Christmas Day.

1500 Old Towne Rd. | West Ashley
(843) 852-4200
www.charlestowne.org

Answer to Did You Know p 34.

If you said Wooly Mammoth you are right! Often, dredging in the boat channel and Charleston Harbor turns up the large, flat teeth of the plant eating Wooly Mammoth. While Charles Town Landing doesn't have a Wooly Mammoth to visit, you can learn about all the other animals that once roamed our shores.

EDISTO ISLAND SERPENTARIUM

This is the first true serpentarium in South Carolina. Exhibits include both exotic and local breeds. Wander through the outdoor gardens and see turtles bask in the sun next to the ponds. Step inside to the solarium and see tropical snakes, tree frogs, and baby alligators.

Daily and Ongoing Events:

Daily programs include dispelling myths and learning facts about snakes, offered at 11 a.m., 1 p.m., 3 p.m., and 5 p.m., and feeding the alligators at 12 p.m. and 4 p.m.

Admission: $12.95/Adult (13+), $11.95/Senior (65+), $9.95/Child (6 – 12), $5.95/Youth (4 – 5). Children 3 and under are FREE.

Hours: Apr. 30 – May 23 Thurs., Fri., Sat. 10 a.m. – 6 p.m.; May 25 – Aug. 15 Mon. – Sat. 10 a.m. – 6 p.m.; Aug. 17 – Sept. 5 Thurs., Fri., Sat. 10 a.m. – 6 p.m. Open Labor Day. Closed Sundays. Closes for the winter the day after Labor Day through mid-Apr.

Directions: From downtown Charleston take Hwy. 17 South approximately 19 miles to Hwy. 174. Turn left and head toward Edisto Island. You will find the Serpentarium 18 miles later on the left.

1374 Highway 174 | Edisto Island
(843) 869-1171
www.edistoserpentarium.com

JEREMIAH FARM and GOAT DAIRY

Jeremiah Farm is a family farm with a raw milk goat dairy, a flock of laying hens, a few rabbits, and large gardens. Jeremiah Farm is dedicated to providing families the opportunity to share the experience of where food truly comes from. Children and adults can try their hand at milking, cheese making, egg gathering, gardening, cooking and preserving food, and drying herbs. Please call ahead to schedule a farm visit.

Tim and Casey Price
Platt Rd. | Johns Island
(843) 559-1678
www.jeremiahfarm.com

SOUTH CAROLINA AQUARIUM

Opened in 2000, the South Carolina Aquarium's many exhibits reflect the state of South Carolina from the mountains in the upstate to the sea in the Low Country. Walk through the upstate's Mountain Forest, peer through the waters of a stream, and see trout feeding and river otters playing. Reach into the Touch Tank and explore sea urchins, horseshoe crabs, and sea stars.

Daily and Ongoing Events:

As you enter the Aquarium you will see a signpost highlighting special activities of the day. The following events are an example of the exciting opportunities that await you at the South Carolina Aquarium:

Breakfast with the Penguins — 9:30 a.m.
Brunch with the Otters — 10 a.m.

Ocean Explorations — 11 a.m.
Touch Tank Feeding — 12 p.m.
Animal Encounters — 1:30 p.m.
Behind the Scenes Tours — 2:30 p.m.

Admission: $17/Adult (12-61), $16/Senior (62+), $10/Child (2-11).
Toddlers (up to 12 months) are FREE.

Hours: Daily Mar. – Aug. 9 a.m. – 5 p.m.; Sept. – Feb. 9 a.m. – 4 p.m. Closed
Thanksgiving Day Christmas Day, but open on Christmas Eve 9 a.m. – 1
p.m.

100 Aquarium Wharf | Charleston
(843) 720-1990
www.scaquarium.org

TIEDEMANN PARK NATURE CENTER

On the upper peninsula of Charleston, you will find the quiet
neighborhoods of Mazyckborough and Wraggborough. In the
late 1700s, well-to-do businessmen built a community in the
pastures that once housed the "Liberty Oak," the grand tree
under which the Sons of Liberty held their pre-Revolutionary
War meetings. The area has become a collection of Greek-
and Georgian- Revival and Victorian homes, coupled with a
Neoclassical church and a Second Presbyterian church. Most of
the homes have been restored, and several museums are now
located within this historic district along Charleston's Museum

Mile. Tiedemann Park is tucked away behind the Charleston Museum in the historic Mazyckborough/Wraggborough neighborhood. Tiedemann's main focus is environmental education for school children, but it offers an array of programs for the public as well. It's well worth trying to participate in one of these programs, as kids have the opportunity to handle reptiles, snakes, and other small animals under the supervision of City of Charleston environmental educators. Events vary by month, are usually on a Saturday, and are FREE unless otherwise noted. Please call in advance to make reservations.

Daily and Ongoing Events:

Reptiles – January 16, 10 – 11:30 a.m.
Busy Bees – January 30, 10 – 11:30 a.m.
Marine Touch Tank – February 27, 10 – 11:30 a.m.
Naturally Green – March 13, 10 – 11:30 a.m.
A Day For Ducks – April 24, 10 – 11:30 a.m.
    (This program is held at Hampton Park.)
Kid's Island Exploration – May 1, 9:30 – 11 a.m.
    (This program is held at Bellinger Island on Daniel Island.)
Shark Study – May 15, 10 – 11:30 a.m.
    (This program is held at Demetre Park.)

Incredible Insects – August 28, 10 – 11:30 a.m.
Reptiles – September 11, 10 – 11:30 a.m.
Huck Finn Fishing Festival – September 25, 9 – 11 a.m.
    (This program is held at Colonial Lake, $3/Child age
    4-12).
Terrific Turtles – October 16, 10 – 11:30 a.m.
Web Weavers – October 30, 10 – 11:30 a.m.
Gobble and Glue – November 20, 10 – 11:30 a.m.
Holiday Nature Crafts – December 11, 10 – 11:30 a.m.

City of Charleston Environmental Education Division
38 Elizabeth St. | Charleston
(843) 965-4002
www.charlestoncity.info/dept

ACTIVITES FOR ALL

One of the first things my parents did after arriving at our usual campsite was to turn us loose — whether for their sanity or ours is still up for debate. We would descend upon the Blue Mountains in rural Pennsylvania with fervor after being cooped up in the car for hours. The remainder of our vacation was then spent running through the woods, climbing trees, tearing around on our bikes, ice skating, sledding, and just generally getting dirty. This chapter is dedicated to all my favorite experiences from childhood. Hopefully, these activities will cement your Charleston vacation in the memory of your family for years to come.

Get outside and enjoy the Low Country. History isn't always found in a museum. You might see that being active will teach you just as much as a museum will. Plus, with all that fresh air and physical activity, you are almost certainly guaranteed a sound night's sleep.

Kayaking

When the United Nations declared 2002 the "International Year of Ecotourism," areas like the Low Country were more than willing to jump on the bandwagon. Of course, Low Country residents have long been living alongside some of the most beautiful marshlands and waterfront areas of the state, or at least we residents like to think. As more and more visitors have, recognized the area as an ecotourism destination, our existing companies have expanded their offerings, and many new outfitters emerged as well. In recent years, people taking to the rivers, ocean and backwaters in kayaks has been on the rise. Our waterways are readily accessible, and there are wide ranges of paddling opportunities available. Guided tours and lessons are plentiful, as are outfitters, with rental prices ranging from hourly to overnighters or even longer. The fee includes the necessary gear to get out on the water safely. You would be wise to call ahead of time to reserve your gear and a tour if you are traveling with a large group; however, it is not mandatory for individuals or a small (3- to 4-member) family to do so.

BOHICKET BOAT ADVENTURE & TOUR COMPANY

Wadmalaw Island is a rural community south of Charleston. Tourism on the Island is virtually non-existent, but for those in the know, activities abound. Paddle through its salt marshes, creeks, and the North Edisto River Basin. Private tours and seasonal kayak rentals are available.

Guided Kayak Tour:
3-hour guided kayak tour $60/Person (5 person minimum). Shuttle runs extend paddle time and distance (and save your muscles) $15/Person.

Kayak Rentals:
Single:
$15/1 hr.
$30/2-4 hrs.
$95/1-2 days.
$125/3-5 days.
$150/Wk.

Double:
$25/1 hr.
$40/2-4 hrs.
$95/1-2 days.
$125/3-5 days.
$150/Wk.

Departure times are based on the tides, so call in advance.

2789 Cherry Point Rd. | Wadmalaw Island
(843) 559-3525
www.bohicketboat.com

COASTAL EXPEDITIONS

In addition to renting kayaks to experienced paddlers, Coastal Expeditions offers kayak tours for any skill level. Guides can also create customized private group tours for families, school groups, churches, and corporations. Coastal Expeditions offers five different locations to disembark on tours: Shem Creek in Mt. Pleasant, the Isle of Palms Marina on the Isle of Palms, Folly Beach at Crosby's Seafood on Folly Road, the Bull Island Ferry in Awendaw, and Carolina Heritage on the Edisto River in Canadys, SC.

Single Kayak Rentals:
$38/Half day (up to 4 hours).
$48/Full day (up to 24 hours).

Double Kayak Rentals:
$48/Half day (up to 4 hours).
$58/Full day (up to 24 hours).

Hours: Daily 9 a.m. – 6 p.m. Cooler temperatures and fewer visitors slow down the desire to kayak for some; from Dec. to Feb., please call ahead to make sure tours and rentals are available.

Shem Creek Maritime Center
514-B Mill Street | Mt. Pleasant
(843) 884-7684
www.coastalexpeditions.com
info@coastalexpeditions.com

KAYAK CHARLESTON

Mr. Earhart's published guidebook, Kayak Charleston, details the innumerable put-ins and public landings around Charleston as well as must-see destinations. Utilizing the tours outlined in his guide, Mr. Earhart offers tours for various group sizes.

Guided Tour Rates:
$30/2 – 2-1/2 hr. tour.
$55/3 – 3-1/2 hr. tour.
$70/5 – 6 hr. tour.

Hours: On demand.

Ralph Earhart
1591 Holton Place | Charleston
(843) 509-3037
www.kayakcharleston.net

Go Local Charleston's
Must See Sites

Ages 2 - 5
Barrier Island Eco Tours

Ages 6 - 9
Stono River Stables Trail
Rides and Camps

Ages 10 - 14
James Island County Park
Climbing Wall

MIDDLETON PLACE OUTDOOR CENTER

The upper Ashley River was once a main waterway serving the plantations that flourished along its banks. Much of the ecosystem has been preserved, and paddlers can explore the salt marsh, swamp, and local flora and fauna on a day trip, sunset tour, and special seasonal tours run by instructors from Middleton Place. Visitors need not be guests of Middleton Inn to participate.

Kayak Tour Rates:
Tour prices range from $12/Person to $65/Person by the hour, and discounts are available if you plan on visiting Middleton Place in addition to the Outdoor Center. Reservations are recommended, so call before making the drive.

Hours: Guided tours 9 – 11 a.m. Self-guided rentals daily 9 a.m. – 3 p.m.

4300 Ashley River Rd. | Charleston (Hwy. 61)
(843) 266-7492
outdoor@middletonplace.org
www.middletonplace.org

NATURE ADVENTURES & CANOE OUTFITTERS, INC.

Departing from various locations in and around Charleston, Nature Adventures offers tours with professional naturalists and instructors. Guided tours are offered daily, ranging from two hours to full day and overnight expeditions.

Guided tour fees:
2 – 2.5 hr. tour, 2-3 miles of paddling: $39/Ages 13+, $29/12 and under.
3 – 3.5 hr. tour, 4-5 miles of paddling: $55/Ages 13+, $39/12 and under.
5 – 6 hr. tour, 5-9 miles of paddling: $85/Ages 13+, $48/12 and under.

Hours: Daily Feb. – Oct. 7 a.m. – 7 p.m.; Nov. – Jan.. 8 a.m. – 5 p.m.

1 Seafood Ln. | Mt. Pleasant
(843) 928-3316 or (800) 673-0679
www.KayakCharlestonSC.com

PADDLEFISH KAYAKING

Paddlefish Kayaking offers guided kayak tours as well as guided boat tours at four locations: Downtown Charleston, Folly Beach, Kiawah Island, and Seabrook Island. Tours are on-demand and by appointment. Tickets may be purchased online.

Rates: Packages start at $30/Person.

(843) 330-9777
www.paddlefishkayaking.com

SEA KAYAK CAROLINA

Spend the morning on the Folly River, or spend the day exploring our barrier islands. Sea Kayak Carolina offers classes with certified instructors on topics such as basic strokes and maneuvers, and introduction to sea kayaking and rolling (your kayak). Guided tours depart daily, and pricing is based on at least 4 paddlers signing up for the tour. If you are interested in a more specific destination, Sea Kayak Carolina will schedule you for a customized trip to Bird Key, Deveaux Bank, or a paddle up the Intracoastal Waterway (ICW).

Rental Rates:
Half day guided tours 3-4 hrs starting at $56.
Full day guided tours 5-6 hrs starting at $90.

Hours: Mon. – Sat. 10 a.m. – 6 p.m., Sun. 10 a.m. – 4 p.m. Tuesday the shop is only open by appointment.

1731 Signal Point Rd. | Charleston
(843) 225-7969
www.seakayakcarolina.com

TIME OUT SPORT & SKI

Time Out is centrally located on Hwy. 17, making kayak rental a quick diversion off the main road. All rentals include paddles, life vests (PFDs), safety gear, and vehicle tie downs for loading your kayak on top of the car, allowing you to get the boat out of the parking lot and to the water.

Rental Rates:
$45/Day – single.
$55/Day – tandem.

Hours: Mon. – Sat. 10 a.m. – 6 p.m., Sun. 12 – 4:30 p.m.

675-A Johnnie Dodds Blvd. | Mt. Pleasant
(843) 388-6266
www.timeoutsports.net

SURFING, PADDLEBOARDING, WATERSKIING, AND KITESURFING

Although only first observed in 1777 by British sailors, surfers in the South Pacific had been riding the waves for generations. In the 1960s, surfing was popularized by Hollywood's beach party movies like "Gidget." The fever spread like wildfire, and now people can surf on cruise ships and in the middle of Arizona! In Charleston, we don't have to go to those extremes. Folly Beach's "Washout" is the main surfing spot, although other beaches, like Isle of Palms, draw surfers as well. Surfing's cousin, both in heritage and style of riding, stand up paddle boarding, or SUP, is all the rage in Charleston these days. Paddlers stand atop an oversized surfboard ranging from 9 to 18 feet long and propel themselves forward with an extended canoe paddle. From a distance, paddlers appear to be standing on the water's surface. Waterskiers of all ages can find rentals on Isle of Palms or Folly Beach. You can kneel or stand, use one or two skis. If you are a newbie, like me, be prepared to spend a good deal of time in the water rather than skiing across it. Kitesurfing requires a bit of practice and is definitely geared toward the older child and teen, or the young at heart parent. It is exactly what it sounds like: you surf as if wind surfing, only you are attached to a kite skating along the water's surface. It's quite the spectacle, but looks like a lot of fun!

Many of the board shops in town offer rentals and lessons, but here are a few you can research in advance of your trip that have online resources.

AIR

Air is a full service kite shop in Charleston with equipment for all your kitesurfing needs, including lessons and rentals. Classes range from "the essentials," to "beyond basics," and are topped off with "special events" for the very experienced kiteboarder.

The following is a basic schedule of class dates (times vary with tide):

The Essentials:
Kite Zen, the most basic level – Mon., Fri., Sat.
Core Basics A, B - Wed., Fri., Sat.
Board Balance - Tues., Thurs., Sat.

Beyond Basics:
Skill Booster – on demand.
Air Support – Tues., Thurs. 3 p.m.

Rates: Lessons start at $149/Person.

Hours: Mon. – Fri. 10 a.m. – 6 p.m., Sat. 10 a.m. – 4 p.m., Sun. by appt.

1313 Long Grove Dr. | Mt. Pleasant
(843) 388-9300
www.catchsomeair.us

CHARLESTON WATERSPORT OUTFITTERS

Charleston Watersport Outfitters carries the largest assortment of rental equipment in the area. If you are new to any watersport, Charleston Watersport Outfitters can set you up with lessons on stand up paddleboarding, kayaking, and surfing. Kayak lessons are $40/hour, and equipment can be rented at an additional fee. Stand up paddleboard and surfing lesson pricing varies, although they start at $50/hour, so call in advance to set up a time and check on rates.

Did You Know?

Did you know that "The Edge of America" can be found right here in Charleston? What is the official name for this popular destination to which locals flock to get their surfing fix?

Find the answer on page 55.

Rental Rates:
Kayak: $40/24 hrs., $30/Additional days, $60/Weekend.
Surfboard: $25/24 hrs., $120/Wk.
Stand Up Paddleboard: $50/24 hrs., $40/Additional days.

Delivery fee for the above rentals is $10 to either Mt. Pleasant, IOP, or Sullivan's Island.

Hours: Mon. – Sat. 10 a.m. – 6 p.m., Sun. 1 – 4 p.m.

1547 Johnnie Dodds Blvd. | Mt. Pleasant
(843) 884-9098
www.charlestonwatersport.com

FOLLY BEACH WATERSPORTS

If you want to frolic in the coastal waters, but aren't sure how to paddle a kayak, ride a surfboard, or get dragged behind a boat on a waterski, chances are Folly Beach Watersports can get you out on the water and teach you some tricks to get you going. The company offers kayak tours, boat charters, parasailing, kiteboard lessons, surfing lessons, jet ski rental, wakeboarding and sailboat rides. All lessons are by appointment, so call when you have the hankering.

Fishing/boat charters: Prices range from $150/2-hr. eco tour to $525/5-hour offshore/near shore fishing trip.

Guided Kayak Tours:
$45/Person – 2 hrs.
$95/Person – 3 hrs.

Parasailing: $60/Person – 600 ft.
$80/Person – 800 ft.

Kitesurfing Lessons: $150/Person – 2 hrs. (incl. equipment and gear).

Surfing Lessons:
$100/Person (private) – 2 hrs.
$75/Person (2-4 people) – 2 hrs.
$310/Person – 5 day surf camp (incl. surfboard and gear).

Jet Ski Rental:
Single Rider- $90/Hr or $60/Half-hr.
Double Rider - $110/Hr. or $75/Half-hr.
Triple Rider - $130/Hr. or $90/Half-hr.

Wakeboarding: $300/Trip up to 6 people (incl. all equipment and instruction as needed) – 2 hrs.

Sailboat Rides: $60/Ride – 1 hr.

(843) 588-3000
www.fbwatersports.com

H2OSMOSIS SPORTS and H2OZ TRAINING CENTER

Hidden away on a secluded lake on Johns Island is the training facility for H2Osmosis Sports. If you are interested in learning how to waterski, this is the place to learn. Coaching instruction can be as little or as much as you wish, and you can rent the lake by the hour or even boat with a captain and equipment if you are so bold. Call in advance for more details and to get directions to the center on Trophy Lake. Equipment is provided if you do not bring your own.

Coaching by the Set: $65/Person – 15-20 mins.
Coaching by the Day: $175/Person – 3 sets (15-20 mins/set).
Weekly Package: $775/Person – Five Days of Skiing.
Lake Rental: $165/Hr – includes boat, driver, instructor and equipment.
Ski/Wakeboard/Rec Rides: $37 – For the experienced riders – each ride lasts 15-20 mins.

Hours: Mon – Fri 9 a.m. – 6 p.m.

PO Box 1108 | Johns Island
(843)793-4470
www.h2osmosis.com

ISLAND BIKE & SURF SHOP

Riding around on Bohicket Rd. can be hazardous if you bring the children; however, just down the road on Wadmalaw Island, you will find Rockville, a sleepy little village of only a few hundred residents. Cruise over the dirt roads and down to Cherry Point Boat Landing. Fish off the pier or buy your own locally caught fish straight off the boat at the shrimp docks you'll see along the way.

Answer to Did You Know p 52.

Folly Beach, otherwise known as "The Edge of America," is Charleston's surfer haven, as well as one of the most laid back places in the county. "The Washout" created by 1989 Hurricane Hugo makes for the best surfing conditions on the island.

Surf board rental: $20/Day; $15/Day if more than 5 days.

3665 Bohicket Rd. | Johns Island
(843) 768-1158 and (800) 323-0579
www.kiawahislandbikerental.com

OLI NAH (Floyd's)

Located on the barrier island of Isle of Palms, Oli Nah (known as "Floyd's" to the locals) carries different boards, SUP, surf, kite, and windsurf equipment in varying sizes.

Rates:
Kitesurfing: Trainer Kite - $25/day, Trainer Kite Lesson (including kite) - $100/First hr., $50/each additional hr., Beginner Lesson (you already have trainer kite experience) - $350/4-hrs., $175/Each additional 2 hr lesson.

Surf and SUP: $50/24 hrs., $30/same day.

Custom deals can be worked out for multiple days.

Dan Floyd, Owner
1204 Palm Blvd. | Isle of Palms
(843) 696-0174 and (843) 886-2723
www.olinah.com

WWW.PALMETTOSURFERS.NET BLOG

This is a surfer's blog site, but it offers a lot of helpful information and links to locals who offer lessons. Also of great importance, it has links to the Folly Surf Cam, the tide tables, and wave reports.

SOL SURFERS SURF CAMP

Sol Sufers Surf Camp is an official Billabong surf camp with several other well known brands as sponsors, including Smith Optics and PowerBar. Professional surfer Kai Dilling offers lessons starting at $75/hr. The longer summer days give rise to summer surf camp. Sol Surfers offers a 5-day group camp for children ages 8-15.

1170 Lazy Ln. | Mt. Pleasant
(843) 881-6700
www.solsurfers.net

SKATEBOARDING

Ah, skateboarding. It's probably the most portable of the board sports. It is still as popular today as it was when my older brothers were busy breaking their bones. Back then, we didn't wear helmets and pads. You had better remember them now, or you won't be allowed to skate at the parks. Besides, wearing safety gear is the smart thing to do.

ACKERMAN PARK

Operated by the City of Charleston, Ackerman Park is in the Sycamore neighborhood of West Ashley. It is open year round, from dawn until dusk, at no charge. This is a public park, so you'll need to bring your own equipment.

55 Sycamore Dr. | Charleston
(843) 724-7321
www.charlestoncity.info

MOUNT PLEASANT SKATE PARK

Skaters need to bring their own gear (helmets, elbow guards, and knee pads). No inline skates, bikes, or scooters are allowed at the park. All park users must sign a registration form and a waiver. While the park is open to all ages, participants under the age of 9 must be accompanied by an adult 17 years of age or older. Call for park hours, days of operation, and further information.

Rates:
Mt. Pleasant resident member annual fee $25.
Non-Mt. Pleasant resident member annual fee $30.
Mt. Pleasant resident member daily user fee FREE.
Non-Mt. Pleasant member daily user fee $3.

Hours: School Year (Aug. – May) - Mon. - Fri. 4 – 630 p.m., Sat. 12 – 5 p.m.; Summer (Jun. and Jul.) - Mon. - Fri. 1 – 5 p.m., Sat. 12 – 5 p.m.

(Behind the R.L. Jones Center)
391 Egypt Rd. | Mt. Pleasant
(843) 856-2196
www.mtpleasantrec.com

THE PARK $

From my (adult) friends, I hear this is THE park for skaters. The Park is an indoor skate park with numerous ramps, jumps, and half-pipes. You'll see a lot of grown-ups there, but kids are also welcome. A summer skate camp last year was pretty successful, and while no information was available at the publication date of *Go Local Charleston*, check back with our website (or The Park's site) for details as they emerge.

Rates: $7/Person except for the following specials:

2 for Tuesday: 3 – 8 p.m. - $10/2 people, 8 – 9 p.m. - $7/2 people.
Old Man Wednesday: 6 – 9 p.m. $3 (this might not be the best time for the youngest of skaters, as there will be adults having the occasional beer — whether you want to expose your children to that is your call.)
Thursday: $7 entry, but FREE lessons from 6 – 8 p.m.
Fri, Sat, Sun: $10 entry.

Hours: Mon. - Thurs. 3 p.m. – 9 p.m., Fri. 3 p.m. – 11 p.m., Sat. 12 – 11 p.m., Sun. 12 – 8 p.m.

4791 Trade St. | North Charleston
(843) 278-4855
www.skateparkofcharleston.com

HORSEBACK RIDING

How much farther off the beaten path can one get than on a horse? Horseback riding opportunities are plentiful in the Low Country. Acres of untouched woodlands and trails still exist on the outskirts of downtown. Most visitors completely overlook this timeless pastime, yet it is a great way to spend time enjoying wildlife. Most stables offer an array of services; some offer protective headgear, but confirm this detail at the time of your reservation.

FOX FARMS
(Arnold C. Fox, Owner and Operator)

Mr. Fox offers beginner, intermediate, and advanced fast rides along a scenic wooded trail. Call ahead of your visit to make a reservation. You are welcome to bring lunch or a snack to enjoy at the farm.

5263 County Line Rd. | Ravenel
(843) 530-1979 and (843) 571-4362
www.foxfarmsllc.com

MIDDLETON PLACE EQUESTRIAN CENTER
The Inn at Middleton Place

Whether you are a guest of the Inn or just visiting for the day, Middleton Place welcomes all experience levels to ride the historic trails along the Ashley River. Protective headgear and riding instruction are provided with the trail ride.

Hours: Trail rides are offered Mon. – Sun. 10 a.m., 11:30 a.m., 1 p.m., 3 p.m. at $45/Person. The recommended minimum riding age is 10, and children must be accompanied by an adult.

4300 Ashley River Rd. | Charleston
(843) 556-8137
www.middletonplace.org

SEABROOK ISLAND EQUESTRIAN CENTER

While Seabrook is primarily a residential island, closed to public access, the equestrian center is open to the public. All skill levels are welcome for guided trail rides, pony rides, or lessons. When you call to make your reservation, you will need to give a credit card number. Once the ride is secured, an Equestrian Center pass will await you at the gate to Seabrook Island.

Rates:
Beginner Trail Ride: $65/Hour per rider.
Advanced Trail Ride: $70/Hour per rider.
Beach Ride (must be a rider with 2-3 yrs. of experience): $95/Rider.
Pony Ride (Parent Led) for children up to 8 yrs.: $40/Half hr.

Hours: Jan. - May, Sept. - Dec.
Beach Ride: Daily 10 a.m.
Beg. or Adv. Trail Ride (Based on skill level) Daily 10 a.m., 1:30 p.m.

Pony Rides: Daily 9 a.m. – 3 p.m.

Hours: Memorial Day – Labor Day.
Beach Ride: Mon. – Sat. 8 a.m.
Beginner Trail Ride: Mon. - Sat. 10:30 a.m., 1:30 p.m.
Advanced Trail Ride: Mon. - Sat. 9 a.m.
Pony Rides: Daily 9 a.m. – 3 p.m.

3772 Seabrook Island Rd. | Seabrook
(843) 768-7541
www.discoverseabrook.com

STONO RIVER STABLE

Owned and operated by G. Marion Reid since 1969, Stono River Stable is a 300-acre working horse farm nestled just seven miles south of Charleston. The facility has a cross-country event course with 63 jumps, miles of private trails, and four riding rings for the experienced equestrian.

Rates: $55/Person for a 1-hr. guided ride.

Hours: Trail rides are available Mon. – Sat. 10 a.m., 1 p.m., 3 p.m., Sun 1:30 p.m.

2962 Hut Rd. | Johns Island
(843) 559-0773 and 1 (800) 777-8951
www.stonoriverstable.com

Therapeutic Riding

Horseback riding has long been used as therapy for those with disabilities. If you are traveling with a family member with special needs, it's important to find activities that suit their needs as well. The following two riding centers offer a riding experience specially catered to children with special needs.

ENCHANTED ACRES EQUESTRIAN CENTER

Summerville
(843) 224-7773
EnchantedAcresHorses@yahoo.com

REIN AND SHINE THERAPEUTIC RIDING

Rein and Shine Therapeutic Riding provides children with physical, mental, and emotional disabilities the opportunity to ride and work with horses. In operation since 2001, Rein and Shine is certified by the NARHA (North America Riding for the Handicapped Association). Since so much evaluation goes into each student, trail rides are not recommended as a one-time event, but rather as a series of visits. If you have a special needs child and are interested, summer camps are offered each year. The website is very helpful, and Katie is the direct contact should you have any questions.

5220 Bedaw Farm Dr. | Awendaw
(843) 849-0964
www.reinandshine.org
admin@reinandshine.org

Rock Climbing

HALF-MOON OUTFITTERS

One wouldn't normally consider an outdoor shop to be a destination for a family outing, but Half-Moon is an exception. The newest of the eight locally-owned, award-winning, and socially-conscious Half-Moon stores boasts an indoor climbing wall. Built to suit all levels of experience (including our 2.5 year old daughter, who scaled it like a monkey), the wall is a great way to spend an hour or so. Half-Moon provides staff to train you on belaying and bouldering skills that you will need to have a successful climb.

Important Notes: All minors ages 13 and under must be accompanied by an adult. Waivers can be filled out at the store or downloaded ahead of time. Birthday parties are given at the wall as well, which closes the wall to the public for the duration of the party. Other basic rules apply, but none need mentioning here, as they don't preclude a trip to the store.

Equipment Rentals: Climbing shoes $2, although street shoes are allowed. Street shoes MUST be closed toed; Harness $3.

Climbing Cards: Climbing cards are a great deal for families. Everyone can use the same card instead of paying for each activity individually. $60/20 punches per card. For example, one day of bouldering per climber is $4, or one punch and one hour of belay and auto belay per climber is $8, or two punches.

Staff-supervised activities are a great way to get a feel for climbing. You'll need to call ahead of time to make an appointment. $12/30-minute belay and bouldering with a staff member (three punches), $16/1 hr. belay and bouldering with a staff member (four punches).

If you have climbing experience and have a belay certification card, you can work the course on your own. However, if you do not have a belay card but are interested in working towards one, Half-Moon offers a belay certification course which is offered twice a month and teaches the correct techniques for belaying, spotting, tying knots, and fashioning climbing equipment. The certification is $12 (three punches).

Bouldering course: $4/Day of bouldering (one punch), $8/Day of belay and auto belay (2 punches).

Climbing Wall Hours: Mon. 3 – 5:45 p.m., Wed. – Fri. 3 – 5:45 p.m., Sat. 12 – 5:45 p.m., Sun. 12 – 4:45 p.m. Closed Tues.

94 Folly Rd. | Charleston
(843) 556-6279
www.halfmoonoutfitters.com

THE CLIMBING WALL AT JAMES ISLAND COUNTY PARK

At 50 feet tall, the Climbing Wall brought to you by Charleston County Parks and Recreation (CCPRC), is the tallest outdoor climbing facility in South Carolina. No climbing experience is required, and the staff is available to assist you. All climbers must fill out a "hold harmless" agreement ensuring that participants are aware of the potential dangers of rock climbing. Belayers must be at least 14 years old. If you plan on being in town for a while, CCPRC also offers a belay certification program, a three hour introduction course which will get the participant familiar with tying knots as well as working with the harness and belying techniques.

The Bouldering Wall is only ten feet tall and provides another location for honing climbing skills without having to worry about harnesses and belaying.

Although the annual, three month and ten climb passes will get you a great financial deal over the repeated purchase of a day pass, they are not transferrable. You can purchase the passes online, at the gate entrance to the park, or by calling the main office. If you happen to have a Greenbax Card (the Piggly Wiggly "VIC" card), you can redeem your Greenbax for a discount on the passes, which is a pretty good deal, and a great way to get rid of those points you aren't really using.

Rates:
$12/Non-resident day pass, $10/Charleston County resident day pass.
$2/Shoe rental (street shoes are allowed, must be closed toes).
$3/Harness rental.
$1/Chalk bag (optional).
$250/Non-resident annual adult, $170/Non-resident annual youth (13 and under).
$190/Charleston County Resident annual adult, $140/Charleston County Resident annual youth.
$110/Non-resident 3-month pass, $90/Charleston County resident 3-month pass.
$95/Non-resident 10-climb pass, $85/Resident 10-climb pass.

Hours: Labor Day – Memorial Day: Closed Mondays, except advertised holidays; Memorial Day – Labor Day Open 7 Days.

Jan. – Feb.: Mon. – Fri. 12 – 5 p.m., Sat., Sun. 9 a.m. – 5 p.m.
Mar: Mon. – Fri. 12 – 6 p.m., Sat., Sun. 9 a.m. – 6 p.m.
Apr: Mon. – Fri. 12 – 7 p.m., Sat., Sun. 9 a.m. – 7 p.m.
May – Aug: Mon. – Fri. 12 – 8 p.m., Sat., Sun. 9 a.m. – 8 p.m.
Sept: Mon. – Fri. 12 – 7 p.m., Sat., Sun. 9 a.m. – 7 p.m.
Oct: Mon. – Fri. 12 – 6 p.m., Sat., Sun. 9 a.m. – 6 p.m.
Nov. – Dec.: Mon. – Fri. 12 – 5 p.m., Sat., Sun. 9 a.m. – 5 p.m.

861 Riverland Dr. | James Island
(843) 795-4386
www.ccprc.com

TIME OUT SPORT & SKI

When Time Out moved from its former home on the downtown Charleston Waterfront a few years back, the new Mt. Pleasant location presented the community with another opportunity to rock climb. The larger store now has an indoor climbing wall, a 40-ft. wall with four stations.

Rates: $8/30 mins., which includes safety equipment. Saturdays can be busy, so call ahead to check for availability, as the wall only has four climbing stations.

Hours: Mon. – Sat. 10 a.m. – 6 p.m., Sun. 12 – 4:30 p.m.

675-A Johnnie Dodds Blvd. | Mt. Pleasant
(843) 388-6266
www.timeoutsports.net

Paint Ball

PAINTBALL CHARLESTON

If tearing around a field loaded down in armor and wielding a weapon that shoots paint balls, is your child's (or your) idea of fun, then Paintball Charleston will make your dreams come true. Located in North Charleston, Paintball Charleston encompasses 60 acres. You can bring your own equipment if you like, and the Paintball Charleston staff will calibrate it for safety, or you can rent the company's gear. Waivers are necessary before participation.

7100 Cross County Rd. | North Charleston
(843) 552-1115

Bike Shops and Rentals

CHARLESTON BICYCLE COMPANY
– Swim, Bike, Run

Charleston Bicycle Company is tucked in amongst the strips of stores lining Hwy. 17. It is THE place for cyclists, runners, and triathletes, and has an excellent selection of bikes and gear for your cycling needs. When driving to the shop from downtown Charleston, look for the store on the left; you'll know you found the right place when you see the enormous bike mounted to the side of the building. If you miss the turn, you'll end up at Krispy Kreme. If you succumbed to eating the doughnuts you will then surely need to rent a bike to work off those delicious calories. Road bikes, hybrids, and cruisers are all available to rent.

Rental Rates:
Road Bikes: $45/Day.
Hybrid Bikes: $8/Hr., $35/Day, $80/Wk.
Cruisers: $6/Hr., $27/Day, $50/Wk.

Hours: Mon. – Fri. 10 a.m. – 6 p.m., Sat 10 a.m. – 5 p.m., Sun. 12 – 5 p.m.

1319 Savannah Hwy. (Hwy. 17) | West Ashley
(843) 571-1211

334-M East Bay St. | Charleston
(843) 407-0482
www.charlestonbicyclecompany.com

ISLAND BIKE & SURF SHOP

Island Bike can be found on the outskirts of Kiawah and Seabrook Islands. Bike rentals are their specialty, but you can rent jogging strollers, Burley trailers, and cargo trailers as well. A lot of vacationers ride bikes on the beach, and it isn't as difficult as you would think. If you are visiting the Shop to rent a bike, why not take a refreshing dip at Beachwalker County Park just down the road on Kiawah Island after your ride?

Did You Know?

Did you know that driving accounts for 20% of carbon emissions each year? Why not reduce your carbon footprint by riding a bike around town instead of driving? Name the bike company that was founded 20 years ago when the term "carbon footprint" was hardly known.

Find the answer on page 71

Bikes can be rented online, by calling the store in advance of your arrival, or by walking into the store. If you are interested in a specific model or style, call in advance for the rental rate.

Rental Rates:
Island Cruisers, Trail-a-Bike, kid's bikes, and joggers: $12/Day, $32/3 Days, $34.95/Wk.
Tandem Bike: $17/Day, $47/3 Days, $52.95/Wk.

Hours: Mon. – Fri. 9 a.m. – 5 p.m., Sun. 9 a.m. – 2 p.m.

3665 Bohicket Rd. | Johns Island
(843) 768-1158 and (800) 323-0579
www.kiawahislandbikerental.com

MIKE'S BIKES

Owner Mike recommends that you call in advance for bike rentals. Should you decide to rent a bike after you have already settled in and don't feel like driving to the shop to pick up your cruiser, Mike's Bikes will deliver rented bikes for free to the beaches when two or more bikes are rented for a week or more. If you are looking for more direction—like where to ride, fun trips or other biking tips—Mike's Bikes' employees are well versed and very helpful.

Rental Rates: $5/Hr; $15/Day, $40/Wk.

Hours: Mon. – Fri. 9 a.m. – 6:30 p.m., Sat. 10 a.m. – 5 p.m., Sun. 12 – 5 p.m.

808 Folly Road Blvd.| Charleston
(843) 795-3322

709 Coleman Blvd. | Mt. Pleasant
(843) 884-5885
www.mikesbikescharleston.com

THE BICYCLE SHOPPE

For over 20 years, family-owned The Bicycle Shoppe has been serving the Charleston community. The Bicycle Dealer Association named The Bicycle Shoppe one of the top 100 bicycle shops in the country with the largest inventory and a comprehensive service department. The Bicycle Shoppe is also known for its environmental role as an advocate of commuting via bicycles and has an extensive webpage with tips, routes, and information for those who are interested in learning how to reduce dependence on driving. If you are just interested in renting bikes and know what you want to rent before you even arrive in town, call ahead to the Shoppe, and they will have your bikes, joggers, trailers, tag-a-longs, and helmets ready for you or ready to be delivered to your house.

Answer to Did You Know p 69.

The Bicycle Shoppe is Charleston's oldest bike shop – 20 years! The Bicycle Dealers Association has named it one of the best 100 bike shops in the country. Stop in and see what you can do to help reduce your impact on the environment.

Downtown In-Store Rental Rate:
Cruisers: $8/Hr., $32/Day, $55/Wk.
Hybrids: $10/Hr., $40/Day, $100/Wk.

Kiawah, Seabrook, Wild Dunes, Isle of Palms, and Sullivan's Island Rental Rate (with free delivery and pick-up): $24/2 days, $30/3 days, $42/week

Hours: Mon. - Fri. 9 a.m. – 7 p.m., Sat. 9 a.m. – 6 p.m., Sun. 1 – 5 p.m.

1539 Johnnie Dodds Blvd. | Mt. Pleasant
(843) 884-7433

280 Meeting St. | Charleston
(843) 722-8168
www.thebicycleshoppecharleston.com

Chartered Boat and Fishing Trips

If you find yourself just aching to get out on the water but would rather have a motor to propel you along, chartered boats are readily available. You can go fishing, sightseeing, or just cruise the waterways. Several companies will let you rent a boat, while others will send a guide along with you for a truly chartered affair. It is customary to tip anywhere between 10 and 15 percent at the end of the trip.

BARRIER ISLAND ECO TOURS

Barrier Island's tours are centered around an island called Capers, a preserve located on the Intracoastal waterway near Isle of Palms. Capers Island is known for its great fishing, bird watching opportunities, and primitive camping (you can find more details about hiking on Capers Island in "Greenspaces, Trails, Reserves, and Parks" on page 85). On the oceanfront-side beach, the sand is littered with fallen trees that are adding to the erosion on the island. Known as "boneyard beach," this section of front beach draws the lens of many photographers.

Scheduled trips led by Barrier Island include a three and one-half hour boat cruise through the tidal creeks, followed by free exploration on Capers Island, kayak adventures around Capers, blue crab excursions where you learn how to catch, clean, and cook your blue crabs, and a five hour long family boat trip with a naturalist-guided walk that includes plenty of time for fishing, relaxing, or collecting shells, with a picnic lunch provided. Many other trips are available, and most trips can be taken year-round.

Barrier Island Eco Tours can also get you to some of the best fishing spots in the area. Choose from 3, 6, or 12- passenger boats and hit the creeks during the Spring and Fall in search of trout, flounder, or shark! If you want to be a bit more adventurous customize your chartered trip to include a fish fry, surf fishing, or fly fishing. Fees include all bait, tackle, and any fishing licenses that are required by law.

Rates: Scheduled trips range in price from $30 - $90/Adult, $22 - $75/ Child 12 and under. Children 2 and under are FREE. Reservations for all trips are required.

50 41St Ave. | Isle of Palms
(843) 886-5000
www.nature-tours.com

BOHICKET BOAT
ADVENTURE & TOUR COMPANY

Bohicket Boat is located at Cherry Point Seafood, where you can rent a boat, take a guided kayak tour, take an in-shore or off-shore fishing trip, cruise on the Pirate's Lady, and get fresh from the ocean seafood—all in one trip! Children 3 and under are FREE on all tours.

Rentals:
Jon boats: Starting at $60.
17' – 22' boat: Starting at $95.
23' boat: Starting at $140.

Private Boat Tours up to 6 passengers starting at $240.

Hours: Daily 8 a.m. – 7 p.m. during the summer season. Off-season hours vary on demand.

2789 Cherry Point Rd. | Wadmalaw Island
(843) 559-3525
www.bohicketboat.com

BOHICKET CREEK BOAT RENTALS

Bohicket Creek Boat Rentals depart from Bohicket Marina on Seabrook Island. The marina is open to the public and has several nice restaurants and shops in addition to boat rentals. From dolphin watching and fishing to sunbathing and shell collecting, renting one of Bohicket Creek's GPS-guided Sea Pros will help you enjoy the waters off Johns, Wadmalaw, Kiawah, and Seabrook Islands.

Rentals: Boat rentals start at $180 and include a fishing license for everyone on board.

Bohicket Marina and Yacht Club
Andell Bluff Rd. | Seabrook Island
(843) 768-1280

COASTAL ECO TOURS

Located on the Intracoastal Waterway, Coastal Eco Tours specializes in private and customizable boat tours. An average tour departing from Isle of Palms lasts three hours. Ride the Salty Dog to Caper's Island for play and relaxation, take a sunset tour, or test your hand at crabbing. If you are just looking for a quick ride out to a quiet and pristine beach, the Caper's Express is for you at a flat $95/hr. Call or visit the website to make reservations.

Rates (tours are limited to 6 passengers):
Capers Island: $295/3 hrs.
Sunset: $195/2 hrs; $295/3 hrs.
Crabbing: $295/3 hrs.

PO Box 62 | Isle of Palms
(843) 886-8136
www.coasteco.com

CAPT. RICK HIOTT'S
INSHORE FISHING CHARTERS

Capt. Rick is an acclaimed charter captain, having recieved awards from the Trident Fishing Tournament for Outstanding Charter Boat Inshore, Outstanding Ecology Award for Offshore Charter Boat, Lowcountry Angler of the Year, and has been featured on the Discovery Channel-Europe. Needless to say, Capt. Rick can help you get out on the water and enjoy a day of fishing for Bull Red Drum, Trout, Flounder, Sheepshead, Spanish Mackerel, and King Mackerel. All fishing tackle and licenses are provided, however you are welcome to bring your own tackle.

Rates (Pricing for 1 - 3 people, add $50 for the 4th person):
$350/4 hrs.
$450/6 hrs.
$550/8 hrs.

Hours: Reservations are required.

(843) 412-6776, (843) 554-9386, and (800) 437-0433
rlhiott@att.net
http://rlhiott.home.att.net

ISLAND BREEZE TOURS

Island Breeze Tours is located on Seabrook Island, a private residential island south of Charleston at the Bohicket Marina which is open to the public and has several nice restaurants and shops in addition to boat rentals. The "Island Breeze" boat takes regularly scheduled cruises with exquisite views of the Bohicket Creek, the North Edisto River Basin, and the surrounding Barrier Islands. You can escape the heat by stepping below to an air-conditioned cabin, and still enjoy the views. Tours require a 10 person minimum, so call in advance before you make the drive.

Rates: $25/Adult, $15/Child (4-12). Children 3 and under are FREE.

Hours: Mon., Wed., Fri. 6 p.m. The tour lasts 2 hours.

Bohicket Marina and Yacht Club
Andell Bluff Rd. | Seabrook Island
(843) 768-1280
www.islandbreezetours.com

SANDLAPPER WATER TOURS

Sandlapper Tours' boats can be seen cruising the Charleston Harbor and her neighboring creeks year round. A diverse variety of tours (up to 49 guests on the 45-foot US Coast Guard Certified catamaran) is available: learn about Charleston's wildlife, sneak up on a Snowy Egret, and float next to Dolphins on a "Nature Tour," listen to stories about Charleston's heritage as you view our steeple-speckled skyline on the "History Tour," and get spooked out with intriguing stories of pirates and lost treasures on the "Ghost Tour." Combine your Bulldog Walking with a Sandlapper boat tour for special rates. Visit the website for schedule of tours or to make reservations.

Rates: Advance ticket purchase recommended.
Boat tour: $15-25/Person.
Bulldog Walking Tour Combo: $40/Adult, $20/Child (4 – 12).

Hours: Daily late Mar. - Oct. 31.

Concord St. at Charleston Maritime Ctr. | Charleston
(843) 849-8687
www.sandlappertours.com

SCHOONER PRIDE

The Schooner Pride is an 84-foot classic tall ship offering up to 49 guests a two hour relaxing day or sunset sail. You can even try your hand at hoisting the sails before kicking back to enjoy historic Charleston Harbor. Visit the website or call for the sail schedule and to make reservations. The Schooner Pride is US Coast Guard Certified.

Rates:
Day Sail: $27/Adult, $23/Child.
Sunset Sail: $37/Adult, $27/Child.

360 Concord St. at Aquarium Wharf | Charleston
(843) 722-1112
www.schoonerpride.com

YARD BOY CHARTERS

Yard Boy Charters is a family-friendly charter for either in-shore or off-shore fishing. Everything else you need to fish is provided for you, including complete rigging, set up and bait. However, you are responsible for sunscreen, food, and drinks. If you're not up for a fishing trip, nature cruises are also available.

Rates:
In-Shore fishing charters: $375 to $550/4 passengers.
Off-Shore fishing charters: $650 – $1400/6 passengers.
Sunset cruises: $200/Minimum 2 hrs.

Fuel cost fluctuations can cause rates to change.

Captain John Walpole
Bohicket Marina and Yacht Club
Andell Bluff Rd. | Seabrook Island
(843) 696-0792
www.yardboycharters.com

GREENSPACES, TRAILS, RESERVES, AND PARKS

Put on your running shoes, hop on the bike, grab your binocs and bug spray, and hit the trails. I've included here a dizzying network of trails and greenways that link the states of the East Coast, take you on a promenade through town, or lead you so far off the beaten path that you feel like you've found your own private Eden.

Neighborhood parks are often overlooked. Why not extend a lunch or snack stop with a park visit? While I have not listed all parks in this guide, I have highlighted those with playground equipment, athletic fields, and picnic areas. Some even have bathrooms!

Regardless of your destination, it is important to remember a few items that will make your trip more enjoyable: bug spray, sun screen, snacks, plenty of water, proper dress, comfortable shoes (not sandals), local flora/fauna guide, and emergency contact information (found at the end of this guide).

Many trailheads post signage that will give a brief description and map of the area, the trail, and the flora and fauna you will encounter on your trek. Pay attention to the pictures of the wildlife, as you are sure to encounter some of them along the way—South Carolina has over 40 different kinds of snakes, though only six are poisonous: eastern diamondback rattlesnake, timber rattler, pigmy rattler, coral, cottonmouth, and the copperhead. Give them a wide berth. You stand to encounter alligators. Don't be fooled by their sluggish appearance, and keep a safe distance. Do NOT feed them either. Do not swim near them. Be smart and don't let children or pets get closer than 60 feet. Alligators are speedier than you would imagine.

Interpretive trails offer stopping points with descriptions of your surroundings or history of the area along the trail. You should be aware that several of our trail networks also serve as hunting grounds during the year, so check with the trail manager or the map at the trailhead. In general, hunting season opens in mid-August, but the various hunting seasons go in and out until February.

As always, respect nature. Leave no trace. Stay on marked trails. If you are taking your dog, s/he must be leashed at all times.

Greenspaces, Trails, and Rserves

AUDUBON SWAMP AT FRANCES BEIDLER FOREST

Difficulty: Easy.
Distance: 1.75 mi.
Terrain: Boardwalk through Swamp.
Use: Hiking only.

The Audubon Swamp is quite a distance outside of Charleston, but it is well worth the drive, as it will take you to the oldest stand of virgin bald cypress and tupelo gum trees left in the world. Many trees have been dated at 1,000 years old. The boardwalk leads you deep into the swamp, so be prepared for wildlife all around. During my last visit, I encountered a Great Horned Owl just a foot away, sitting on the handrail staring at me. Too cool.

Daily and Ongoing Events:

Groups of 10+ can arrange for a guided tour $7/Person.

Rent canoes $8/Person.

Night walk schedule (not for children under 10): $8/Person.
January 23 - 5 p.m.
February 27 – 5:30 p.m.
March 27 – 6 p.m.
April 24 – 7:30 p.m.
May 22, Jun. 26, Jul. 24 – 8:30 p.m.
August 21 – 8 p.m.
September 18 – 7:30 p.m.
October 23 - 7 p.m.
November 20 – 5:30 p.m.
Dec. 18 – 5 p.m.

Admission: $7/Adult (non-Audubon mems); $6/Adult (Audubon mems); $3.50/Child (6-18). Children under 6 are FREE.

Hours: Tues. – Sun. 9 a.m. – 5 p.m. Closed New Year's Eve, New Year's Day, Thanksgiving, Christmas Eve, and Christmas Day.

Directions: Take 1-26 West to exit 187. Follow the signs for "Beidler Forest."

Mims Rd. | Harleyville
(843) 462-2150
www.beidlerforest.com

BEAR ISLAND WILDLIFE MANAGEMENT AREA

Difficulty: Easy.
Distance: 5 miles.
Terrain: Dirt, grass, marsh.
Use: Day hiking only.

While Bear Island is a worthwhile hiking destination, its real attraction lies in the wildlife viewing more than the walking. Bald eagles, wood storks, wintering waterfowl, osprey, hawks, heron, shore birds, and song birds all frequent the area. Observation platforms and dikes provide the visitor with ample locations to view wildlife.

Admission: FREE.

Hours: Daylight in designated areas from Feb. 9 – Oct. 31. The area is closed from Nov. 1 – early Feb.

Directions: Located off Hwy 17. Take Bennett's Point Rd (look for the green sign) approximately 13 miles. You'll see the main entrance about a mile after crossing the Ashepoo River.

Titi Rd. | Green Pond
www.dnr.sc.gov/mlands/managedland?p_id=56

CAPERS ISLAND HERITAGE PRESERVE

Difficulty: Easy.
Distance: 5 miles.
Terrain: Sand, beach, maritime forest.
Use: Day hiking only, fishing, boating, primitive camping.

Go Local Charleston's
Must See Sites

Ages 2 - 5
Animal Trail at Charles Towne Landing

Ages 6 - 9
Nature Walk and Bike at Magnolia Plantation

Ages 10 - 14
Cape Romain National Wildlife Reserve

Capers Island is located just behind Isle of Palms on the Intracoastal Waterway. The island is only about three miles long and one mile wide. It is a popular kayak and boat destination for the locals, and you can only access it with a floatation device. A camping permit alerts the park managers of your presence and enables you to stay overnight. If you don't have a camping permit, you have to leave an hour before sunset to ensure your safe arrival back at the main land before nightfall. The McCaskill Trail is a must-do for birders.

Admission: FREE.

Awendaw
843-953-9300
www.dnr.sc/gov/mlands/managedland?p_id=666

CAPE ROMAIN NATIONAL WILDLIFE REFUGE

Difficulty: Easy.
Distance: "Bull Island NRT" 2 mi, "Sheephead Ridge" 3.7 mi, "Old Fort Loop" 6.6 mi.
Terrain: Dirt, sandy roads.
Use: Day Hiking, canoeing/kayaking.

The barrier islands of the Low Country were once home to numerous Native American tribes, including the Edisto, Ashepoo, Combahee, Cusabo, and Kiawa to name only a few. The area north of Charleston to the Santee River was once home to the Sewee Indians. As one of the barrier islands, Cape Romain was established as a migratory bird refuge in 1932. It comprises 22 miles of barrier islands, salt marshes, coastal waterways, impoundments, and maritime forest. It is a main battleground in the preservation of the threatened loggerhead sea turtle.

Cape Romain Lighthouse, built in 1827, stands 65 feet tall, and in its heyday was visible from 14 miles during favorable conditions. Thirty years later, a 150-foot lighthouse was built, adding a second light that was visible for 19 miles and is

Did You Know?

Did you know the original bridge spanning the Cooper River, known as the Grace Memorial, was constructed in 1929? In 1966, the Silas Pearman Bridge was built to parallel the existing bridge and expand capacity. The need for a safer, larger, and taller bridge never ended, so in 2005, this bridge replaced the out of date bridges.

Find the answer on page 90

credited for saving many ships from wrecking. Both lighthouses are on the National Register for Historic Places and are now non-operational. The lighthouses are located in a wilderness area, and access is limited.

Neighboring Bulls Island is also part of Cape Romain National Wildlife Reserve. This 5,000 acre island will surely fill your day. Wildlife here is plentiful, and if you look closely enough, you will see white-tailed deer, alligators, otters, raccoons, black fox squirrels, reptiles, and amphibians galore. Of course, migrating birds are what the island is best known for. Be sure to walk along the beach on the northeast corner of the island, for it is a testament to the power of nature and the ever-changing shape of barrier islands. Littered with fallen trees, the sands are slowly eroding the island away in one spot, while depositing the sand and building the island up in another. Also of interest are Martello Tower and Old Fort. These towers were lookouts used to warn against the approach of pirate ships.

Please note that no pets are allowed on the islands. You may only collect a small bag of dead shells. You can also saltwater fish, provided you abide by state regulations.

Barrier Island Refuge is accessible only by boat/ferry. Coastal Expeditions runs a ferry service and is the exclusive concessionaire of Cape Romain. For more information about Coastal Expeditions, see "Activities For All" on page 47 or call them at (843) 884-7684. The Bull Island Ferry is $30/Person. It runs Tues., Thurs., Fri., and Sat. from Mar. to Nov. The rest of the year it runs on Saturdays only. Call (843) 881-4582 for the schedule.

CRAB BANK SEABIRD SANCTUARY

While not really a hiking trail, Crab Bank is a beautiful sandspit island to paddle past if you are in the area. Just off Shem Creek, it is a destination point for many kayak outfitters in the area, as it is easy to reach. At just about 22 acres (as it naturally changes shape and size), the island is utilized as a nesting ground to brown pelicans, terns, black skimmers, snowy egret, and many other sea and shorebirds.

Admission: FREE.

Hours: Closed to the public from Mar. 15 – Oct. 15 for bird nesting, the island and its feathered inhabitants are still visible from your boat. From Oct. 16 – Mar. 14, visitors can walk the shores below the high tide waterline.

Charleston Harbor | Mt. Pleasant
www.dnr.sc.gov/mlands/managedland?p_id=215

DONNELY WILDLIFE MANAGEMENT AREA

Difficulty: Easy.
Distance: "Backwater" 1.5 mi, "Boynton" 3 mi.
Terrain: Dirt, grass, short boardwalks, and bridges.
Use: Day Hiking, biking, no vehicles allowed.

Donnely is another amazing wildlife area with joint management by South Carolina Department of Natural Resources, Ducks Unlimited, the National Wild Turkey Federation, the United States Army Corps of Engineers, the Nature Conservancy, and several other local conservation groups. The area is composed of wetlands, managed rice fields, forested wetland, tidal marshes, and a natural stand of longleaf pine—once a major source of shipbuilding wood in the early days of South Carolina. During your visit, you will have great songbird and migratory bird watching – you might see turkeys, dove, and waterfowl. Other animals, like the white-tailed deer and alligators, also call Donnely home, but they are not seen often by the day hiker.

Admission: FREE.

Hours: Daylight, but closed for special hunts. Visitors are required to register at the kiosk at the main gate near Hwy 17. Boynton Nature Trail is closed Nov.1- Feb. 9.

Directions: Take Hwy 17 S past Walterboro. Immediately north of the 17/ SC 303 junction, turn right onto the gravel road. The WMA office is .5 mile on the left. The parking area is on the left before the kiosk.

585 Donnelley Dr. | Green Pond
https://www.dnr.sc.gov/mlands/managedland?p_id=58

DUNGANNON HERITAGE PRESERVE

Difficulty: Easy.
Distance: 9 mi.
Terrain: Dirt, grass, short boardwalks, and bridges.
Use: Day Hiking, biking, no vehicles allowed.

Formerly a freshwater reserve for a plantation, Dungannon is now home to one of the top nesting colonies of wood storks. In South Carolina, the wood stork is protected by the Federal government as an endangered species. Wood storks nest in concentrated populations called rookeries from April to June. While rookeries are mostly found in standing swamp water atop tall cypress trees, no walking is allowed in the nesting area.

Along the trail through the upland forest, keep your eyes open for the wild boar tracks. They dig around in the soft mud, upturning roots, small plants, and rocks, looking for food. Because Dungannon is 643 acres, you might also see deer, migrating waterfowl, songbirds, snakes, and alligators.

Admission: FREE

Hours: Daylight, year round

Directions: Take Hwy 17 to Rantowles. At the fork with the gas station, turn across traffic. Go southeast on Hwy. 162 for about 6 miles. Dungannon's entrance is on the right. Park at the gate and sign in and out.

Hwy. 162 | Hollywood
www.dnr.sc.gov/mlands/managedland?p_id=120

EAST COAST GREENWAY

The East Coast Greenway spans nearly 3,000 miles from Canada to Key West. It is a developing system of trails for walking, biking, and hiking that weaves in and out of all the major cities on the Eastern seaboard, including Charleston. In the Low Country, you'll find the trail taking you through neighborhoods as well as through wooded trails. The West Ashley Greenway is part of

Answer to Did You Know p 86

The Arthur Ravenel Bridge now stands where the Grace Memorial and Silas Pearman bridges once stood. It is the longest cable-stayed bridge in North America at 1546 feet. Each year, runners from around the world gather in Apr for the Cooper River Bridge Run. But you don't have to wait all year to walk or ride the bridge; locals and tourists alike do it every day.

the network of trails.

http://www.greenway.org/sc.php

West Ashley Greenway (WAG)

Difficulty: Easy.
Distance: Charleston Route 22 mi; Mt. Pleasant Route: 32 mi.
Terrain: paved streets, dirt trails, mostly flat (except for the Cooper Bridge, of course).
Uses: Day Hiking, biking (use a mountain bike for the Inland Route).

The Island Route: Not only will you get in a lot of exercise on this walk/ride, you'll also get a good dose of sightseeing. The WAG consists of two linked routes, though you can stop wherever you choose. The Island Route begins at the Charleston Maritime Center in the heart of downtown Charleston and takes you across the Arthur Ravenel, Jr. Bridge (known to locals as the New Cooper River Bridge), the longest cable-stayed bridge in the Western Hemisphere. From the peak of the bridge, you'll be able to see Charleston, Mt. Pleasant, Sullivan's Island Lighthouse, Castle Pinckney, the Atlantic Ocean, and the nation's fourth largest port system—the Port of Charleston. Once over the bridge, turn right for a side trip to Patriots Point Museum. Should you choose, instead, to go straight down Coleman Blvd., you will cross scenic Shem Creek Bridge and enter through the Old Village of Mt. Pleasant. Weave through neighborhoods to get a glance at Charleston Harbor. As you make your way down Coleman Blvd., you will cross the Ben Sawyer swing bridge over the Intracoastal Waterway and enter Sullivan's Island. Isle of Palms is also connected by sidewalks, and both beach islands are well worth the visit – plus, after all that walking and riding, you'll probably be ready for a meal and a dip in the ocean!

The Inland Route: Beginning at White Point Gardens in downtown Charleston, you will leave the Battery heading south through the historic district. The large waterfront and hundreds of years- old houses will be interesting to adults and older kids, but probably not so much the youngest ones. If you are not traveling with young children or are not worried about riding next to high speed traffic, take either the Ashley River Bridge on Lockwood Dr. or the James Island Connector. If you are wary of the traffic, use the South Windermere Shopping Plaza as your starting point. Located on Folly Road Blvd. just across from the Ashley River Bridge, South Windermere is the home of the natural food store Earth Fare – the giant tomato on the store sign is a surefire indicator you are in the right neighborhood. Ample parking is available. Behind the strip of earth-conscious stores, you'll find the WAG trailhead. Once the hike begins, you will again weave through neighborhoods, parks, and saltwater marshes. The end of the trail is at the base of Limehouse Bridge and Main Road on Johns Island.

ERNEST F. HOLLINGS
ACE BASIN NATIONAL WILDLIFE REFUGE

Difficulty: Moderate.
Distance: 3 mi loop.
Terrain: Dirt trails, marsh, fields.
Use: Day Hiking only.

The ACE (Ashepoo, Combahee and South Edisto) Basin National Wildlife Reserve (NWR) is one of the largest estuaries left undeveloped on the East Coast of the US, consisting of 11,815 acres over four counties. The basin is broken into two units and is a joint venture of the US Fish and Wildlife Service, the South Carolina Department of Natural Resources, The Nature Conservancy, and Ducks Unlimited. The Edisto Unit (7,200 acres) is the closest access point to Charleston, at just around an hour's drive from downtown Charleston.

Tidal marsh, wetland impoundments, bottomland hardwoods, upland forests, and grass and shrub lands await the day hiker. Kids will love the open expanse and the opportunity to get muddy while observing nesting bald eagles, migrating ducks and waterfowl, raptors, and songbirds. Tucked away amidst all nature's beauty is the Grove Plantation, a land grant from 1694. Over the years, the property changed hands; then in 1828, George Washington Morris built the plantation house. The Grove House, as it later became known, is one of three plantation houses in the basin to survive the Civil War. It was purchased by the Nature Conservancy in 1991.

IMPORTANT NOTE: Hunters use this land as well as hikers: September – November is deer hunting season, while November – January is waterfowl hunting season. Always check with headquarters by calling in advance if you are in doubt about the safety of hiking during the season. Normally, one unit is closed for hunting while the other remains open for hikers.

Hours: Daily, daylight to dark. When the front gate is closed, visitors are allowed to park and walk in. Grove Plantation is open to tours Mon. – Fri. 7:30 a.m. – 4 p.m.

Directions: Take Hwy. 17 South to SC 174. The signage here is helpful and says "Edisto Beach" and "ACE Basin National Wildlife Reserve." Turn right at the intersection on to Willtown Rd. Travel approximately 2 miles. The entrance to the NWR is on the left. The Plantation House is another 2 miles down a gravel road.

Hollywood/Edisto Unit
www.fws.gov/acebasin

FRANCIS MARION NATIONAL FOREST

This forest has historical significance as the military icon, Francis Marion, also known as the "Swamp Fox," disrupted British supply lines during the Revolutionary War by preying on the British soldiers' fear of alligators and snakes. Never having encountered alligators or snakes in warfare on the British Isles, the soldiers were rightfully frightened by these large, and sometimes lethal, creatures. Prehistoric Indians have also left their mark with a 4,000 year old shell ring. Since the devastation in 1989 by Hurricane Hugo, Francis Marion National Forest has been recreating herself. You'll still see the remains of the storm in blown over trees and a thick understory of re-growth. Keep an eye out for the endangered red-cockaded woodpecker! The following pages (96-99) offer detail of the many trails in the forest.

5821 Hwy. 17 N | Awendaw
(843) 928-3368
www.fws.gov/seweecenter/francismarion

AWENDAW PASSAGE OF THE PALMETTO TRAIL
(In the Francis Marion NF)

Difficulty: Easy.
Distance: 14-mile hike.
Terrain: Dirt trails.
Use: Day Hiking, Mountain Biking.

The Awendaw Passage is the terminal point of the trail, also known as the Mountian-to-the-Sea Trail, which is an easy 7-mile hike. Two trailheads provide access: Buck Hall Recreation Area Trailhead (eastern trailhead) is just 30 miles north of Charleston, and Swamp Fox Trailhead (western trailhead) is 25 miles north of Charleston.

Buck Hall Recreation Area Trailhead

Facilities include public restrooms, drinking water, picnic tables/shelters, developed campgrounds ($15/Tent per night; $20/RV per night), and a boat ramp.

Admission: $5/Vehicle.

Hours: 6 a.m. – 10 p.m.

Directions: From downtown Charleston, take Hwy. 17 North approximately 30 miles. Buck Hall Recreation Area is on the east side of the road. The trailhead itself is a half mile down the road.

Swamp Fox Trailhead

Directions: From downtown Charleston, take Hwy. 17 North approximately 26 miles to Steed Creek Road (SC 1032). Trailhead is on the west side of the road about ¼ mile past Steed Creek Rd. If you are coming from the south, drive past the trailhead and make a u-turn to reach the entry.

I'on Swamp Interpretive Trail
(In the Francis Marion NF)

Difficulty: Easy
Distance: 2 mile loop
Terrain: Unsurfaced, grassy
Use: Day Hiking only

A walk through this swamp takes the visitor back to the time of early European settlers in the 1700s. Interpretive signs point out the embankments and ditches used to make impoundments for rice fields. Today, these fields are no longer in use for rice production, but they offer a great habitat for wildlife. Hunters love the impoundments because migrating waterfowl make pit stops here throughout the season. That said, be sure to read the trailhead and take note of the hunting season. Another note: this is already a swamp, and will become more so after significant rains, so it is not recommended for hiking during such periods.

Directions: Take Hwy. 17 North to I'on Swamp Rd. and turn left. The trailhead is 2 miles down the road on the left.

Sewee Shell Mound Interpretive Trail
(In the Francis Marion NF)

Difficulty: Easy.
Distance: 1 mi.
Terrain: Unsurfaced, grassy.
Use: Day hiking.

This very easy hike offers visitors a look back 4,000 years to the time of the Sewee Indians. Even though the forest was left ravaged by Hurricane Hugo in 1989, the views of the marsh, creeks, and Intracoastal Waterway afford the visitor beautiful scenes of nature as she rebuilds.

Directions: Take Hwy. 17 North to Doar Rd. North. Turn right and look for Salt Pond Rd., approximately 2 miles, then turn right onto FS Road 243. The trailhead is barely a 10th of a mile.

South Tibwin
(In the Francis Marion NF)

Difficulty: Easy.
Distance: 5 mile loop.
Terrain: Unsurfaced, grassy, tall grass, mud, sandy roads.
Use: Day hiking and biking only.

Formerly a plantation, South Tibwin Trail will give the visitor a crash course in Low Country natural and cultural history. Meander past former rice fields, salt water creeks, and maritime forests. Songbirds, raptors, wading birds, bald eagles, and alligators will keep you company on this quick walk.

Directions: Take Hwy. 17 North past the Sewee Visitor and Environmental Education Center, approximately 12.5 miles. While the trail is unmarked, look for the opened iron pipe gate on the right. A parking area and information board mark the trailhead.

Truxbury Horse
(In the Francis Marion NF)

Difficulty: Easy.
Distance: 14 mi of connecting trails.
Terrain: Old railway, dirt/mud.
Use: Day hiking, biking, horseback riding.
Some areas of this trail flood after heavy rains.

Open: Daylight, year round.

Directions: Take Hwy 17 and turn left onto Hwy 41. Drive 7 miles (Just past Wando); the parking area and trailhead are on the left

GIVHANS FERRY STATE PARK

Difficulty: Moderate.
Distance: "Old Loop" 5.4 mi, "River Bluff" 1.5 mi.
Terrain: Dirt with several steep slopes.
Use: Day Hiking only, fishing, boating, camping, picnic.

Part of the Edisto River Canoe and Kayak Trail, Givhans Ferry is a great place for a picnic lunch after a nice family hike. During the summer months, take a dip in the river. Swimming and playing by the waterside is best when water levels are low, at least for the young children. Picnic areas and shelters are available for renting, $25 - $38/Day. No reservations for the shelters are necessary, but it is first-come-first-serve.

You can thank the Great Depression for the creation of Givhans Ferry, as it was built by the Civilian Conservation Corps. The park is also known for its limestone river bluff; (as you've probably noticed, the Low Country is rather flat, so bluffs tend to stand out).

Admission: $2/Adult, $1.25/SC senior. Children age 15 and younger FREE.

Hours:
Apr. - Sept. 9 a.m. – 9 p.m.
Mid Sept. - Oct. Mon. – Thurs. 9 a.m. -6 p.m., Fri. - Sun. 9 a.m. – 9 p.m.
Nov. – Mar. 9 a.m. – 6 p.m.

Directions: From I-26: Take exit 187 onto Hwy 27 towards Ridgeville and go 1 mile to Hwy 78. Take a left and go approximately ¼ of a mile and take a right on Hwy 27. Stay on Hwy 27 for 7 miles to Hwy 61. Take a right on Hwy 61 for 3 miles to Givhans Ferry Road. Turn right and the park entrance is ¼ mile on the left.

746 Givhans Ferry Rd. | Ridgeville
(843) 873-0692
www.southcarolinaparks.com

SANTEE COASTAL RESERVE WILDLIFE MANAGEMENT AREA AND WASHO RESERVE

Difficulty: Easy.
Distance: "Woodland Trail" 1.1, "Bike/Hike" 7.2, "Marshland" 1.9.
Terrain: Dirt, sandy roads, grass-covered dikes.
Use: Day hiking, biking, canoeing/kayaking.

Santee Coastal Reserve consists of several properties: Murphy Island, Cedar Island, The Cape, and Washo Reserve. The 24,000 acres of property is home to migratory and wintering waterfowl, shore and wading birds, white-tailed deer, wild hogs, bobwhite quail, the endangered red-cockaded woodpecker, and songbirds. A 500-foot boardwalk provides an excellent stopping point for bird watching. If you are lucky, you might see the endangered American Swallow Tailed Kite. Good for the bird that citizens and scientists have banded together to monitor their nesting and progress in the hopes of bringing the bird back from the fringe.

The reserve is dappled with hiking and biking trails, as well as canoe trails along the Intracoastal Waterway and South Santee River. The Reserve, now owned by The Nature Conservancy, is one of the largest rookeries for Wood Storks on the East Coast of the US. If you acquire a permit, you can spend the night camping.

The Washo Reserve is included in the Santee Coastal Reserve and features a freshwater cypress lake and swamp. It started off the same as many marsh areas around the state, as a plantation for the production of rice, indigo, and cotton, and like the others, it was decimated by the Civil War and hurricanes. The land was quickly descended upon by hunters and preserved, although still used for hunting. In 1974, the Santee Gun Club donated the land to the Nature Conservancy. These days hunting is permitted only in specific areas and only during scheduled hunting events.

Hours: Open for limited public use year round from 8 a.m. – 5 p.m., except during scheduled hunts Nov. – Jan.

Directions: Take Hwy. 17 North past McClellanville. Approximately 3 miles past McClellanville, turn right onto South Santee Rd. Santee Gun Club Road will be on the right about 3 miles farther down. It is a dirt road leading to the reserve. The information center is another 2.5 miles down the road.

210 Santee Gun Club. Rd. | McClellanville
(843) 546-6062
www.nature.org/wherewework/northamerica/states/southcarolina/preserves/art7316

SAWMILL BRANCH BIKE/HIKE

Difficulty: Easy.
Distance: 6.1 mi loop.
Terrain: Paved.
Use: Day Hiking, biking.

Walk along the Sawmill Branch Canal through the southern part of Summerville.

Hours: Daily during daylight hours.

Directions: Take Hwy. 26 to exit 199 onto Hwy 17A toward Summerville. Drive west into Summerville and turn left onto either Gahagan Rd. or Luden Dr.

Gahagan Rd. or Luden Dr. | Summerville
(843) 871-6000
www.visitsummerville.com

SEWEE VISITOR AND
ENVIRONMENTAL EDUCATION CENTER

Difficulty: Easy.
Distance: "Nebo Pond" 1 mi.
Terrain: Dirt, sandy, paved roads.
Use: Day Hiking, picnic.

Sewee Center is jointly owned by the US Fish and Wildlife Service and the US Forest Service. It provides a central education setting for Cape Romain National Wildlife Reserve and Francis Marion National Forest. There is a live endangered red wolf viewing area, an education and lecture space with special events, and an auditorium with orientation film. Also on site is a bookstore with many helpful guides and educational books for the family.

Hours: Tues – Sat 9 a.m. – 5 p.m. Closed on all major holidays.

5821 Hwy. 17 N | Awendaw
(843) 928-3368
www.fws.gov/seweecenter

SOUTH CAROLINA STATE TRAILS PROGRAM

South Carolina has over a hundred scenic trails. You can wander through neighborhoods or extend a trip to a museum or plantation with an interpretive walk along the riverfront. Many of the trails listed here adjoin historic sites listed in other chapters of *Go Local Charleston*. Here is a list of parks, centers, and historic sites that are associated with SC Trails for your quick reference. If you would like more detail on the trail before your trip, such as a map, the SC Trails website (www.sctrails.net) practically takes you on the hike from your couch!

Edisto Beach State Park | Edisto Beach
       Spanish Mount: 1.7 mi
       Scott Creek: .6 mi
       Big Bay: .4 mi
       Campground: .4 mi
       Forest Loop: .5 mi
       Bike: .4 mi
Charles Towne Landing | Charleston
       Charles Town Landing Garden: .3 mi
       Animal Forest: 1 mi
       History: 1.5 mi
Charleston County Parks and Recreation | Various Locations
       Nature Island (Palmetto Islands CP): 1.2 mi
       Unpaved Nature (Palmetto Island CP): 1 mi
       Paved Bike (Palmetto Island CP): 1.2
       Needlerush Parkway Bike (Palmetto Island CP): 1.2 mi
       Red Loop (James Island CP): 1.4 mi
       Orange Loop (James Island CP): .8 mi
       Blue Loop (James Island CP): 2.2 mi
       Green Loop (James Island CP): 1 mi
       Yellow Loop (James Island CP): 1.5 mi
       Leisure Paved (Wannamaker CP): 2 mi

CAW CAW Interpretive Center | Ravenel
    Swamp Sanctuary: .4 mi
    Upland Forest Loop: .3 mi
    Bottomland/Hardwood Forest: 1.1 mi
    Waterfowl: 1.2 mi
    Marshland: 1 mi
    Maritime Forest: .4 mi
    Rice Fields: 1 mi
    GA Pacific Swamp Boardwalk: >.5 mi
Magnolia Plantation | Charleston/West Ashley
    Nature Walk and Bike: 5 mi
    Magnolia Wildlife: 3.4 mi

SC Department of Parks, Recreation and Tourism
1205 Pendelton St. | Columbia
(803) 734-0173
www.sctrails.net

Neighborhood Parks By District

Most of these parks are great destinations in and of themselves. Have a picnic, find a quiet place to read, or play to your heart's content. We like to hit the parks to break up an otherwise busy day of traveling around town. These stops make the natives in the back seat a lot happier if they can stretch their legs a bit. Daytime access and FREE admission is standard. Spend an hour or stay for the day.

Charleston Peninsula

BRITTLEBANK PARK

Features: play equipment, fishing dock, walking trail, picnic tables.

Lockwood Dr. | Behind "The Joe" Stadium | Charleston
(843) 724-7334
www.charlestoncity.info

HAMPTON PARK AND MCMAHON PLAYGROUND

Features: 1 mile loop for bikers/joggers/walkers, playground, fields, public restrooms, drinking water, and picnic area.

Directions: Go south on Rutledge Ave. and turn right onto Cleveland Street. Cleveland runs straight into the park.

(843) 724-7334
www.charlestoncity.info

HAZEL PARKER PLAYGROUND

Features: Playground, tennis court, picnic area, athletic fields, basketball courts.

70 East Bay St. |Charleston
(843) 724-7334
www.charlestoncity.info

MOULTRIE PLAYGROUND

Features: Playground, tennis courts, and athletic field.

41 Ashley Ave. | Charleston
(843) 724-7334
www.charlestoncity.info

TIEDEMANN PARK

Features: Playground, athletic field, restrooms, educational programs - see Birds, and Fish, and Mammals - Oh My! on page 39.

40 Elizabeth St. | Charleston
(843) 724-7334
www.charlestoncity.info

WATERFRONT PARK

You'll find Waterfront Park and pier along the entry to Charleston Harbor tucked behind the Old Exchange area. It is less of a playing park and more of a sightseeing park in that there is no playground equipment. However, during the warm months, you'll find children and adults frolicking in the large water fountain. This is also a great location for a picnic or a break from all the walking. The walkways are designed with low-lying bushes demarcating quaint "rooms" so you feel as though you have your own private space to relax.

Near Adger's Wharf | Charleston
(843) 724-7334
www.charlestoncity.info

WHITE POINT GARDENS

Also known as "The Battery" or "Battery Park," White Point Gardens stretches along the Ashley and Cooper Rivers to the Charleston Harbor. Some of the oldest and largest of Charleston homes are found just behind the park. While you stare at the homes and wonder how anyone could keep up a house like that, your children will enjoy crawling like ants all over the cannons and cannon balls that line the front side of the park. The elevated walkway provides a view of the Harbor, Castle Pinckney, Fort Sumter, and many other landmarks, like the USS Yorktown.

East Bay St around to South Battery | Charleston
(843) 724-7334
www.charlestoncity.info

Daniel Island

ETIWAN PARK

Features: Playground, athletic fields, picnic area, basketball courts, and public restrooms. The park is relatively new.

453 Seven Farms Dr. | Daniel Island
(843) 724-7334
www.charlestoncity.info

SMYTHE PARK

Features: Picnic areas with grills, walking paths and trails, lake, pirate ship playground.

Daniel Island Dr. | Daniel Island
www.danielisland.com

CHILDREN'S PARK

Features: trails, dock, fishing, playground equipment, shrimp boat playground, picnic area, beach at low tide, water spray fountain, large ground map.

Riverlanding Dr. | Daniel Island
www.danielisland.com

Isle of Palms

ISLE OF PALMS RECREATION DEPARTMENT

Features: Playground, picnic area, athletic fields, basketball court, tennis court, gymnasium, Frisbee golf course, bathrooms.

Hours: Daylight. Gymnasium has its own schedule: Mon. 7 am – 6 p.m., Tues. 7 a.m. – 7 p.m., Wed. 7 a.m. – 8 a.m./9 a.m. – 4 p.m., Thurs. 7 a.m. – 7 p.m., Fri. 7 a.m. – 6 p.m., Sat. 12:30 – 5 p.m., Sun. 1 – 5 p.m.

24 28th Ave. | Isle of Palms
(843) 886-6428
www.iop.net

James Island

JAMES ISLAND COUNTY PARK

Features: Playground, open meadows, picnic areas, restrooms, saltwater fishing and crabbing, seasonal spray fountain, paved walking/biking trails, dog park, sand volleyball court, horseshoe pits, and Splash Zone Waterpark, a seasonal waterpark available for an additional cost. For a full description of Splash Zone, see "Watering Holes" on page 142. Additional amenities not included in admission are a 124-site campground, 10 cottages, bicycle, pedal boat, and kayak rentals, covered shelter rental, and the Climbing Wall (see "Activities For All" on page 65 for more information on the Climbing Wall).

Rates: $1/Person, Children under 2 are FREE.

Hours:
Jan. - Feb. 8 a.m. – 5 p.m.
Mar. - Apr. 8 a.m. – sunset.
May – Labor Day 8 a.m. – 8 p.m.
Sept. - Oct. 8 a.m. – sunset.
Nov. - Dec. 8 a.m. – 5 p.m.

871 Riverland Dr. | James Island
(843) 795-7275 or (843) 795-4386
www.ccprc.com

PLYMOUTH PARK

Features: Playground, picnic tables.

35 Plymouth Ave. | James Island
(843) 724-7334
www.charlestoncity.info

Johns Island

ANGEL OAK

Features: Picnic tables, public restrooms, store.

You won't find a jungle gym at this park, but you will find a live oak tree that will make your eyes glaze over in amazement. The limbs of the tree are not to be used for climbing, but boy, one could have a lot of fun in a tree of this stature. Reportedly 1,500 years old, the Angel Oak (so named for the previous landowners Martha and Justin Angel), is 25.5 ft. in circumference. Its limbs drape and sprawl, creating a labyrinth worth eating your lunch under. There is a sweet gift shop on the premises you should visit as well.

Hours: Mon. - Sat. 9 a.m. – 5 p.m., Sun .1 – 5 p.m.

3688 Angel Oak Rd. | Johns Island
(843) 559-3496
www.angeloaktree.org

JOHNS ISLAND

Features: Playground, athletic fields, tennis courts (the playground can be a bit dirty at times, but that's hit or miss).

1727 Bozo Ln. | Johns Island
(843) 724-7334
www.charlestoncity.info

McClellanville

ROBERT E. ASHLEY LANDING

Features: Picnic tables, playground, boat landing, museum (www.villagemuseum.com).

Pinckney St. | McClellanville
www.townofmcclellanville-sc.net

Mount Pleasant

ALHAMBRA HALL

Features: Playground, picnic tables, drinking water, public bathrooms, historic structures, and views of Charleston Harbor.

131 Middle St. | Mt. Pleasant
(843) 849-2053
www.townofmoutpleasant.com

GREENHILL COMMUNITY CENTER

Features: Activity building, playground, and outdoor basketball court.

Hours: Mon. - Fri. 4 – 7 p.m., Sat. 10 a.m. – 7 p.m.

707 York Street (off Mathis Ferry Road.) | Mt. Pleasant
(843) 856-2172
www.townofmtpleasant.com

MT. PLEASANT PALMETTO ISLANDS COUNTY PARK

Features: Playground, picnic area, walking/biking trails, 50-ft observation tower, open meadows, tidal creek fishing and crabbing dock, dog agility area and dog park, sand volleyball court, horseshoe pits, and, for an additional fee, seasonal Splash Island Waterpark. For a full description of Splash Island Waterpark, see "Watering Holes" on page 141. Additional amenities offered for a fee include bicycle and pedal boat rentals, covered picnic shelters, snack bars, vending machines, and birthday party packages.

Rates: $1/Person. Children under 2 are FREE.

Hours:
Jan. - Feb. 8 a.m. – 5 p.m.
Mar. - Apr. 8 a.m. – sunset.
May – Labor Day 8 a.m. – 8 p.m.
Sept. - Oct. 8 a.m. – sunset.
Nov. - Dec. 8 a.m. – 5 p.m.

444 Needlerush Pkwy. | Mt. Pleasant
(843) 884-0832 or (843) 795-4386
www.ccprc.com

MT. PLEASANT PIER (CCPRC and Town of Mt. Pleasant)

Features: Playground (fenced), fishing, pier, walking trails (paved), restrooms, snack/souvenir shop.

71 Harry Hallman Blvd. | Mt. Pleasant
(843)762-9946 or (843) 795-4386
www.townofmtpleasant.com
www.ccprc.com

PARK WEST COMPLEX

Features: Activity building, 2-court gym, playground, football, baseball, soccer, softball fields, pool, changing room, lake pavilion, multi- purpose field, walking trails, horseshoe pits.

Pool Hours: Mon. - Fri. 7 a.m. – 7 p.m., Sat. 10 a.m. - 5:30 p.m., closed Sun.

1251 Park West Blvd. (off of Hwy 17N.) | Mt. Pleasant
(843) 856-2536 and (843) 856-2196
www.townofmountpleasant.com

REMLEY'S POINT COMMUNITY CENTER

Features: Activity building, playground, outdoor lighted basketball court.

Hours: Mon. – Fri. 3:30 - 6:30 p.m., Sat. 11 a.m. - 5:30 p.m.

363 6th Street (off of Mathis Ferry Rd.) | Mt. Pleasant
(843) 849-2059
www.townofmtpleasant.com

RICHARD L. JONES CENTER

Features: 25-meter indoor heated pool, locker rooms, gym, supervised skatepark, lighted batting cages, playground, softball and athletic field.

Hours: Mon. - Fri. 8 a.m. - 8:30 p.m., Sat. 10 a.m. – 6 p.m.

391 Egypt Road | Mt. Pleasant
(843) 884-2528
www.townofmountpleasant.com

North Charleston

NORTH CHARLESTON PARK CIRCLE
(Next to Felix C. Davis Community Center)

Features: Playground, athletic fields, picnic area, public restrooms (open when Community Center is open), frisbee golf course.

Directions: Take 526 (Mark Clark Expressway) to exit 19/Rhett Ave. Travel approximately 1 mile and you will be at Park Circle

4800 Park Circle
843-745-1028
www.northcharleston.org

NORTH CHARLESTON WANNAMAKER COUNTY PARK

Features: 2 playgrounds, grassy open meadows, dog park, trails, seasonal sprinkler water play, restrooms, snack bar, shaded porch, picnic sites, sand volleyball court, and horseshoe pits. Whirlin' Waters Adventure Waterpark is a seasonal waterpark available for an additional cost. For a full description of Whirlin' Waters see "Watering Holes" on page 142. For a small fee, rent a bike, pedal boat, or kayak.

Rates: $1/Person. Children under 2 are FREE

Hours:
Jan. - Feb. 8 a.m. – 5 p.m.
Mar. - Apr. 8 a.m. – sunset.
May – Labor Day 8 a.m. – 8 p.m.
Sept. - Oct. 8 a.m. – sunset.
Nov. - Dec. 8 a.m. – 5 p.m.

8888 University Blvd. | North Charleston
(843) 572-7275 or 843-795-4386
www.ccprc.com

RIVERFRONT PARK
(At the former Navy Base)

Features: Picnic tables, public restrooms, playground, shelter, walking/biking path, spray fountain (kids love playing in this), fishing pier, and fields.

1001 Everglades Dr. | North Charleston
(843) 740-2699
www.northcharleston.org

Sullivan's Island

SULLIVAN'S ISLAND PARK

Features: Playground, tennis courts, and fenced-in area.

1610 Middle St. | Sullivan's Island
(843) 883-3198

Summerville

GAHAGAN PARK

Features: athletic fields, bathrooms, picnic tables.

515 West Boundary | Summerville
(843) 851-5211
www.visitsummerville.com

West Ashley

MARY UTSEY PLAYGROUND

Features: Playground and shady areas for resting.

1360 Orange Grove Rd. | West Ashley
(843) 724-7334
www.charlestoncity.info

ST. ANDREW'S PARK AND PLAYGROUND

Features: Playground, athletic fields, tennis courts, and picnic area.

1095 Playground Rd. | West Ashley
(843) 763-4360
www.standrewsparks.com

WEST ASHLEY PARK

Features: Public restrooms, playground, picnic tables, trails, and athletic fields.

Bishop Dr. | West Ashley
(843) 724-7334
www.charlestoncity.info

U-PICK IT FARMS, MARKETS, AND LOCAL CATCH

What good is a family outing without a dose of dirt, bug bites, and sunscreen? Charleston is home to many small family farms that are open to the public to participate in a rite of childhood passage: strawberry picking. Most farms listed offer a wide range of crops such as pumpkins, tomatoes, and blueberries for the plucking to give families year-round entertainment. Remember to ALWAYS contact the farm on the morning before you visit to confirm hours, conditions, and availability of the specific crops you wish to pick!

Nearly every day of the week, farmer's markets are held throughout the county. Roadside tents often "crop up" as the harvest season progresses. How much more local can you get?

Seafood is yet another staple in our diet. Recently, the flood of imported shrimp has damaged the local shrimpers. As a result, Charleston is proud to boast a "Friends Don't Let Friends Eat Imported Shrimp" attitude. Look for local catch and markets touting the Sustainable Seafood Initiative.

AMBROSE FAMILY FARM

Ambrose Farm is a transitional farm – meaning it is in the process of moving from traditional farming practices to organic farmingn practices. Though Ambrose follows organic practices, it takes growers several years to upgrade their soil conditions. Farmer Pete has been at it for about 3 years and is having remarkable success. The owners grow, amongst other fruit and veggies, asparagus, beans, blackberries, blueberries, flowers, onions, peas, strawberries, and tomatoes. Local tomatoes are probably one of the best foods you'll eat in your life. If you want to have a farm tour, call ahead of time – the Ambrose's will even make your lunch for you!

Hours: Open for U-Pick Apr. – mid July Mon. – Sat. 9 a.m. – 6 p.m., Sun. 11 a.m. – 5 p.m. (Apr. and May only). Closed all holidays and whenever it is raining (but call before you rule out the farm, as it might be raining where you are but it might be perfectly sunny on Wadmalaw).

The Farm
2349 Black Pond Ln. | Wadmalaw Island
(If your GPS doesn't recognize this address, use Selkirk Plantation Rd. in place of Black Pond Ln.)
(843) 559-0988

Stono Market and Café (run by the Ambrose family with fresh produce, jams, preserves, and sit-down or take-out meals made to order).
842 Main Rd. | Johns Island
(843) 559-9999
www.stonofarmmarket.com

BOONE HALL FARM

Boone Hall (the farming side of Boone Hall Plantation) offers U-Pick strawberries, peaches, tomatoes, and other fruits and vegetables, and it also has Christmas trees in season. There's always something going on at the farm and plantation: picking food, Strawberry Festival, or Halloween hay rides. See "Special Events Calendar" on page 167 for more information about the events at Boone Hall Plantation.

Hours: Mom. - Sat. 9 a.m. - 7 p.m., Sun. 10 a.m. - 6 p.m.

1235 Long Point Rd. | Mt. Pleasant
(843) 856-5366 (Produce and Information)

Boone Hall Market Store & Market Café
2521 Highway 17 N | Mt. Pleasant
(843) 853-8154
http://boonehallfarms.com

Go Local Charleston's
Must See Sites

Ages 2 - 5
Ambrose Family Farm's
Strawberry Season

Ages 6 - 9
Boone Hall Farm's Hay
Rides

Ages 10 - 14
Legare Farm's Amazin'
Maze in Maize

CHAMPNEY'S
BLUEBERRY FARM

On the outer reaches of Charleston County, Champney's offers U-Pick blueberries and pre-picked produce (the non-blueberry produce comes from other South Carolina farms). Only cash is accepted at the farm.

Hours: Mon. - Sat. 9 a.m. – 8 p.m.

4492 Rose Dr. | Ravenel
(843) 763-6564 and (843) 834-1891
champneysblueberries@gmail.com

JOSEPH FIELD'S FARM

Field's organic produce is available at the farmer's markets as well as at a stand on the corner of River Rd. and Maybank Hwy. next to the CVS pharmacy.

Hours: Daily May – August, 8 a.m. – 6 p.m.

3129 River Rd. | Johns Island
(843) 559-3894

Did You Know?

Did you know that South Carolina ranks at or near the top, nationally, on the production of fruits and vegetables? Can you guess what crops are tops from South Carolina?

Find the answer on page 125.

KING'S MARKET

King's Market offers U-Pick blackberries; however, the season is short at around a month, depending on the weather. Also sold at the market is a variety of vegetables, as well as peaches, boiled peanuts, cut flowers, honey, jams, jellies, dressings, pickles, rice, grits, bakery items, and shrubs.

Hours: Open Mar. – Dec.

2559 Hwy 174 | Edisto Island
(843) 869-3600
kingsfarmmarket@aol.com

LEGARE FARMS

Legare (spoken as "Leh-gree") Farms is well known for the "Amazin' Maze in Maize," an activity which leads the visitor over 7 acres, 3 miles of paths of twists and turns, and 5 bridges during October. Summer programs offer children the opportunity to learn the difference between dairy and beef cows and how animals and plants rely on each other for food in the Legare Farms nursery. Families are invited to visit the farm in the winter months as well, when they can feed the animals and play in the playground.

Legare Farms preserves the farm's bounty providing delicious jams, jellies, relishes, pickles, and sauces. These products, along with hormone and antibiotic- free beef, are available at the farm's country store.

Special Events:

Charleston Corn Maze, Hayrides and Pumpkin Picking: A day at Legare Farms can easily be spent enjoying cooler fall weather while wandering amidst the ever-shrinking rural landscape of Johns Island.

Admission: $1/Person, $6/Age 11+ for all day maze, $3/Ages 2 – 11 all day maze. Children under 2 are FREE.

U-Pick Pumpkins: $6/Regular, $8 – 15/Extra large. Hayrides $2/person.

Hours: Fall Festival Oct. Fri. 3 – 10 p.m., Sat. 10 a.m. – 10 p.m., Sun. 1 – 6 p.m.

Fall Harvest Dinner and Meet the Farmer Social – Early Nov. (date to be announced)

Hours: Mon. – Fri. 8 a.m. – 4 p.m.

2620 Hanscombe Point Rd. | Johns Island
(843) 559-0763
www.legarefarms.com

MYERS BLUEBERRIES

U-Pick blueberries. Meyers Blueberry fields are typically open mid-June – July. A recorded message in mid-May will give the exact opening date.

Hours: Mon. - Fri. 7:30 a.m. - 7:30 p.m., Sat. 7:30 a.m. - 2:30 p.m.

206 Twin Lakes Dr. | Summerville
(843) 873-8695

NOELS CHRISTMAS TREE FARM

I'm sure you never imagined Johns Island as a Christmas tree cutting destination, but tucked behind Maybank Hwy. is Noel's Christmas Tree Farm. Leyland Cypress trees await you as you wander through the acres. Kids can take hay rides through the fields while your tree is baled for easy transporting.

Hours: Mon. after Thanksgiving - Christmas. Mon. - Fri. 3 p.m. - dark, Sat. - Sun. 9 a.m. - dark.

Directions: Take Maybank Hwy. across Johns Island and turn at the Noel's Tree Farm sign on Fernhill Rd. Drive until you see the trees.

1665 Fernhill Rd. | Johns Island
(843) 209-9461

Answer to Did You Know p 122

South Carolina is second in the nation for peach production. We rank at or near the top in the production of those healthy leafy greens like spinach and kale that mom always makes you eat. And each year, our tomatoes and watermelons grace the picnic tables of millions of houses nationally.

Buy South Carolina. Nothing's fresher. Nothing's finer.

ROSEBANK FARMS

Rosebank Farm is a quick stop, particularly if you are on your way home from Beachwalker Park, Kiawah or Seabrook Islands. Located on the main road on and off the islands, Rosebank Farm is a market stand that sells local produce, flowers, jams, jellies, art, and seafood.

4455 Betsy Kerrison Pkwy. | Johns Island
(843)768-9139
www.rosebankfarms.com

TOOGOODOO CHRISTMAS TREE FARM

As if decorating a Christmas tree doesn't create enough memories of your children's youth, add to it by cutting your own! Wander through Toogoodoo's fields of Eastern Red Cedar, Leyland Cypress, Virginia Pine, and White Pine. The Farm will provide the saws, shake the tree, and bag it for you. If being environmentally conscious is on the top of your list but you still want a tree, Toogoodoo has potted Leyland Cypress trees as well. Don't feel like cutting a tree and dragging it to the car? The Farm also has a nice selection of precut Fraser Firs. Add to your holiday experience with a winter train ride! Surely after all this fun, you'll need a snack and somewhere to eat, and Toogoodoo Farms has a special refreshment stand, picnic area, and restrooms to suit your needs.

Hours: Open Fri. after Thanksgiving - Christmas. Thurs. – Fri. 2 p.m. – dusk, Sat., Sun. 10 a.m. – dusk.

Directions: Take Hwy 17 South toward Edisto, look for the left turn onto Hwy 165 (it's a merge to the left more than a turn). Follow Hwy 165 for approximately 7 miles into Hollywood. At the only stop light in Hollywood, turn left onto Toogoodoo Rd. After 3 miles you will see the farm on the left.

7355 Toogoodoo Rd. | Younges Island
(843) 475-6445 or (843) 425-3802
www.toogoodootreefarm.com

Farmer's Market

Farmer's markets in the Low Country are the perfect place to spend a morning or evening. With locations spattered across the map, there is always one nearby. Farmers from across the state and neighboring states combine with local artisans and entertainment to provide a spectacular venue to better get to know the locals and what we have to offer. Special events are also listed on the websites of each location's market to further add to the choices of entertainment.

CHARLESTON FARMER'S MARKET

Hours: Open Apr. – Dec., Sat. 8 a.m. – 2 p.m.

Marion Square | Downtown Charleston
www.charlestonarts.sc (follow the links to the festivals and special events)

DANIEL ISLAND FARMER'S MARKET

Hours: Apr. – Sept., Thurs. 3 p.m. – DUSK.

161 Seven Farms Dr. | Daniel Island
Family Circle Tennis Center

FRESHFIELDS VILLAGE

Hours: Jun. – Aug., Mon. 4 – 8 p.m.

Freshfields Village | Johns Island

FOLLY BEACH FARMER'S MARKET

Hours: Thurs. – Sun., 10 a.m. - until it's over.

60 Center St. | Folly River Park

MT. PLEASANT

Hours: May – Oct., Tues. 3 p.m. until DARK.

Coleman Blvd. @ Moultrie Market Pavilion | Mt. Pleasant
www.townofmountpleasant.com

MEDICAL UNIVERSITY OF SOUTH CAROLINA (MUSC)

Hours: Apr. – late Fall, Fri. 7 a.m. – 3 p.m.

MUSC Horseshoe
171 Ashley Ave. | Charleston

NORTH CHARLESTON FARMER'S MARKET

Hours: Mid-Apr. – to Mid-Oct., Thurs. 1 p.m. – 7 p.m.

Park Circle's Felix C. Davis Community Center
4800 Park Circle | North Charleston
(843) 745-1028

SHELMORE VILLAGE

Hours: Mid-Apr. - early Sept., Wed. 4 p.m. until DARK.

732 South Shelmore Blvd. | Mt. Pleasant

SUMMERVILLE FARMER'S MARKET

Hours: Mid-Apr. - Mid-Oct., Sat. 8 a.m. – 1 p.m.

Doty St. (Between Main and Cedar Sts.) | Summerville

Local Catch

Backman Seafood
1851 Sol Legare Rd. | Johns Island
(843) 795-2393

Captain Hatt's Shrimp Market
9988 N. Hwy. 17 | McClellanville
(843) 887-3038

Cherry Point Seafood
2789 Cherry Point Rd. | Wadmalaw Island
(843) 559-0858

Crosby's Seafood
382 Spring St. | Charleston
(843) 937-0029

Crosby's on Folly
2223 Folly Rd. | Folly Beach
(843) 795-4049

Mt. Pleasant Seafood
1 Seafood Dr. | Mt. Pleasant
(843) 884-4122

Raul's Seafood Market
100 Church St. | Shem Creek Mt. Pleasant
(843) 388-8046

Simmons Seafood
1400 Palm Blvd. | Isle of Palms
(843) 886-6449

Stono Farm Market
842 Main Rd. | Johns Island
(843) 559-9999

Wando Shrimp Company
102 Haddrell St. | Mt. Pleasant
(843) 884-9933

Earth Fare
74 Folly Rd. | James Island

Whole Foods
923 Houston Northcutt Blvd. | Mt. Pleasant

WATERING HOLES

Ranging from laid back, fun-loving Folly, to Kiawah's family- friendly Beachwalker Park, there is a beach for every age. Not all beaches have lifeguards posted, so I have pointed out those that do. Lifeguards are posted at County Parks from May through mid-August, seven seven days a week. From mid-August through Labor Day, lifeguards are only posted on the weekends. During the off-season, swimmers enter the water at their own risk.

If the beach doesn't provide enough activity for the young-uns, then Charleston County Parks and Recreation has three water park locations that are sure to please. From baby wading pools to tubes of shooting water, there is plenty of fun to be had. The water park operating schedule is influenced by the local school schedule (June – Labor Day). By May the parks are open on the weekends, but come the first of June, they are open seven days a week. No outside beverages and snacks are allowed.

Beaches

EDISTO BEACH STATE PARK

Edisto Beach is on Edisto Island, and while it is on the outer reaches of all places in this guide, it is well worth the day trip. Approximately 50 miles south of downtown Charleston, Edisto Island and Beach are filled with Low Country charm. Plus, the Serpentarium is a really cool place to take the kids if they like snakes, alligators, and lizards! Hit Caw Caw Interpretive Center on your way there or back. See the "Birds, and Mammals, and Fish – Oh My!" on page 33 for more information.

Amenities at the oceanfront park include hiking and biking trails, boardwalks, campgrounds, an environmental center, a "green" exhibit building, fishing and boating access, a playground, and a park store/gift shop.

Admission: $4/Adult, $2.50/SC Senior, $1.50/Child (6-15). Children 5 and younger are FREE.

Directions: Take Hwy. 17 South to Edisto Hwy./SC-174 and merge to the left. Edisto Hwy. takes you across Edisto Island, past the Serpentarium, and onto Edisto Beach. The State park entrance is on the left as you enter the town.

Hours: Mon. – Sun. 8 a.m. – 6 p.m. (hours are extended to 6 a.m. – 10 p.m. during Daylight Savings Time).

8377 State Cabin Rd. | Edisto Island
(843) 869-2756
http://southcarolinaparks.com/park-finder/state-park/1298.aspx

FOLLY BEACH

Known as the "Edge of America," Folly Beach has its own very laid back attitude. Surfers and sunbathers abound, and there are shops and restaurants in the town center. Walking and bike riding the island are easy, and recommended. From May 1 through September 31, dogs are prohibited unleashed on the beach between 10 a.m. – 6 p.m. Drive down the beach to "The Washout," where Hurricane Hugo split the island in half in 1989 for the best surfing location. Please note that lifeguards are not posted on Folly's beaches, so enter the water at your own risk. Just a bit further down the beach on the north end of Folly Island you will be able to see Morris Island Lighthouse.

Go Local Charleston's
Must See Sites

Ages 2 - 5
Beachwalker Park,
Kiawah Island

Ages 6 - 9
Any of the Waterparks

Ages 10 - 14
Folly Beach

Folly's beaches fill up quickly, so parking can become an issue if you wait to arrive until midday. If you do not choose to use public access parking, follow these basic rules (a complete set is available at www.cityoffollybeach.com): park in the direction of traffic, do not park on the sidewalks, and do not block private or public driveways.

Directions: Take Calhoun Street west to the James Island Connector (Robert B. Scarborough Bridge). Traffic dead ends at Folly Road Blvd, where you will turn left. Travel on Folly Road Blvd. until you reach the beach. Be very mindful of Folly Island speed limits.

OR Take Highway 17 South over the West Ashley Bridge. Merge left with traffic on to Folly Rd. Continue straight on Folly Road Blvd. until you reach Folly Beach.

FOLLY BEACH FISHING PIER

The fishing pier is 7,500 sq. ft. with a full-service restaurant, rod rentals, restrooms, gift and tackle shop, showers, and beach access. Don't feel that you have to fish on the fishing pier; it's a great place to see the sights of Folly Beach and meet some locals.

101 East Arctic Ave. | Folly Beach
(843) 588-FISH (3474)
Folly Beach County Park

FOLLY BEACH COUNTY PARK

Turn right on West Ashley for the County Park, where most traffic will be turning left to search for public access parking. Parking is plentiful and beach access is simple. Most importantly for families, lifeguards are posted during the summer season (ending mid-August). Other amenities include dressing areas, restrooms, picnic area, seasonal retail area, shelter rentals,

---

Did You Know?

Did you know that rip currents account for more than 80% of lifeguard rescues at the beach? Charleston's area beaches post flags and signs in areas prone to rip currents. If you get caught in a rip current and find yourself getting farther away from the beach, do you know how to keep safe?

Find the answer on p 139.

outdoor showers, boardwalks, seasonal snack bar, and seasonal beach chair and umbrella rental.

Admission: $7/Car.

Hours:
Jan. - Feb. 10 a.m. – 5 p.m.
Mar. - Apr. 10 a.m. – 6 p.m.,
May - Labor Day 9 a.m. – 7 p.m.
Sept. - Oct. 10 a.m. – 6 p.m.
Nov. - Dec. 10 a.m. – 5 p.m.

1100 West Ashley | Folly Beach
(843) 588-2426

ISLE OF PALMS

Once a playground for the well-to-do, the Isle of Palms is still quite popular, although it is now a tourist-centered beach more so than any other in Charleston. The main strip on the Isle of Palms houses many shops, restaurants, and public restrooms. The City of Isle of Palms offers beach access and public parking, both metered street side and paid lots for nominal fees. Meters are only enforced during the season (mid-March through early October). Vehicles can be parked on any road, so long as it is not designated as prohibited, and the car must face the direction of the traffic, with all four wheels off the road. No access paths to the beach can be blocked. In addition, should you be traveling with your dog, know that it must be leashed and curbed.

Breach Inlet is the area of tidal flow between Sullivan's Island and Isle of Palms. The current in this area is very swift and, therefore, it is NOT safe for swimming. Please take care that you pay attention to any postings about beach safety.

ISLE OF PALMS COUNTY PARK

The County Park is located immediately off the Isle of Palms Connector. Parking is plentiful and beach access is simple. Most importantly for families, lifeguards are posted during the summer season. Other amenities include dressing areas, restrooms, picnic areas, sand volleyball court, outdoor showers, boardwalks, children's play area, and seasonal beach chair and umbrella rentals.

Directions: Take Hwy 17 North over the Arthur Ravenel Bridge through Mt. Pleasant to the Isle of Palms Connector. Turn right onto the Connector; it will take you directly onto the Island and to the beach.

Admission: $7/Car.

Hours:
Jan. - Feb. 10 a.m. – 5 p.m.
Mar. - Apr. 10 a.m. – 6 p.m.
May - Labor Day 9 a.m. – 7 p.m.
Sept. - Oct. 10 a.m. – 6 p.m.
Nov. – Dec. 10 a.m. – 5 p.m.

Isle of Palms County Park
1 14th Ave. | Isle of Palms
(843) 886-3863

KIAWAH ISLAND BEACH/BEACHWALKER PARK

Beachwalker Park is your only access point to the beach while on Kiawah, unless you are a guest of the resort. This is probably the most family-friendly beach in Charleston, as it is small, and lifeguards are posted during the summer season. Beachwalker's access caters primarily to the summer visitors, so off-season hours are somewhat limited. Parking is plentiful, and beach access is simple. Other amenities include dressing areas, restrooms, picnic area with grills, outdoor showers, boardwalks, seasonal snack bar, seasonal beach chairs, and umbrella rentals. The trip to Beachwalker Park can be filled with side trips like kayak tours, pleasant bike rides, and a promenade through Freshfields Village or Bohicket Marina.

Admission: $7/Car.

Hours:
Mar. - Apr. weekends only 10 a.m. – 6 p.m.
May - Labor Day 9 a.m. – 7 p.m.
Sept/ 10 a.m. – 6 p.m.
Oct. weekends only 10 a.m. – 6 p.m.
Nov. - Dec. the beach is closed. Closed Jan. - Feb.

Directions: Take Hwy. 17 South and follow the Ashley River Bridge, where Hwy. 17 becomes Savannah Hwy. Follow Savannah Hwy. through West Ashley to the Main Rd. intersection. Turn Left onto Main Rd. Cross Limehouse Bridge onto Johns Island. Be aware that Main Rd. becomes Bohicket Rd. at the Maybank Hwy. intersection. Follow Bohicket Rd.

Answer to Did You Know p 136.

NOAA's National Weather Service and National Sea Grant Program have partnered with the United States Lifesaving Association to educate beachgoers on the dangers of rip currents. Follow these tips if you find yourself in a rip current: Don't fight the current. Swim out of the current and parallel to the shore then swim into the shore. If you can't escape, float or tread water. If you need help, call or wave for assistance. Remember, learn how to swim, never swim alone, and "when in doubt, don't go out." For more information on rip current safety, visit www.ripcurrents.noaa.gov.

through the roundabout as you enter Kiawah Island and merge onto the island (which will be on your left). Just before the gatehouse leading onto the resort, turn right on Beachwalker Ave. The county park is at the end of the street.

OR take Hwy. 17 South and cross the Ashley River Bridge. Merge to the left onto Folly Road Blvd. Follow Folly Road Blvd. over the drawbridge and merge to the right onto Maybank Hwy. Cross the Stono Bridge (officially Paul J. Gelegotis Brige) onto Johns Island. At the Bohicket Rd./Maybank Hwy. intersection, turn left. Follow the directions above from Bohicket Rd. to the county park.

SULLIVAN'S ISLAND

Sullivan's Island is a mix of locals and tourists, though it is much more a local's destination. There are only about 2000 residences, no hotels or B&Bs, but homes are still rented during the year to vacationers. Unlike its Isle of Palms neighbor, Sullivan's Island is more untouched, reaturing only a few restaurants and shops. Be sure to see the Sullivan's Island Lighthouse while driving around the island. There are no public parking lots on the island, so arrive early to find on street parking. Specific ordinances dictate that dogs must have a license (available from Town Hall), and leashes must be under 10 feet in length.

No lifeguards are posted on Sullivan's Island, so you must swim at your own risk. As with Isle of Palms, the currents can be very strong at times. Breach Inlet is the area of tidal flow between Sullivan's Island and Isle of Palms. The current in this area is very swift. Therefore, it is NOT safe for swimming.

Dogs are allowed on the beach from November 1 - March 31. During those months, dogs may be off the leash from 5 a.m. – noon, but must be leashed from noon – 5 a.m. From April 1 -

October 31, dogs are allowed off the leash 5 a.m. – 10 a.m. but are not allowed on the beach between 10 a.m. - 6 p.m. From 6 p.m. – 5 a.m. dogs must be leashed.

Directions: Take Hwy 17 North over the Arthur Ravenel Bridge. Exit on Coleman Blvd. Follow Coleman to Ben Sawyer Blvd, which subsequently crosses the Ben Sawyer Bridge and takes you onto Sullivan's Island.

Waterparks

SPLASH ISLAND WATERPARK
(Palmetto Islands County Park)

This waterpark features a 200-ft. water slide, 16-ft. otter slide, sprays, geysers, raindrop waterfalls, The Cyclone (10 minute swirling water ride), recreational pools, lifeguards, concessions/restrooms/showers, and changing areas with lockers. There are also lounge chairs for the grownups who are lucky enough to have children who play independently.

Admission: $7.99/General admission, $6.99/Charleston County Resident, $5.99/Children under 48", $3.99/Senior (60+), $4.99/After 3 p.m. Children ages 2 and under are FREE. Mon. – Fri. large group rates also apply.

Hours: The waterpark opens for the summer based on the school schedule and is open only on the weekends until Jun. If you plan to visit before the first week of Jun., call ahead to check on schedule; otherwise, the waterpark is open daily from 10 a.m. – 6 p.m.

444 Needlebrush Pkwy. | Mt. Pleasant
(843) 884-0832
http://www.ccprc.com/index.aspx?nid=10

SPLASH ZONE WATERPARK
(James Island County Park)

This water park features a 200-ft. tube slide, 200-ft. open slide, Caribbean play structure with slides, wheels, and sprays, 500-ft. lazy river with an adventure channel featuring sprays and a waterfall, leisure pool, concessions, restrooms, and showers/changing areas with lockers. Lounge chairs are available for those who want to relax while the kiddies play.

Hours: The waterpark opens for the summer based on the school schedule and is open only on the weekends until Jun. If you plan to visit before the first week of Jun., call ahead to check on schedule; otherwise the waterpark is open daily from 10 a.m. – 6 p.m.

Admission: $11.99/General admission, $9.99/Charleston County Resident, $8.99/Children under 48", $5.99/Senior (60+), $6.99/After 3 p.m. Children ages 2 and under are FREE. Mon. – Fri. Large group rates also apply.

871 Riverland Dr. | James Island
(843) 795-7275
http://www.ccprc.com/index.aspx?nid=10

WHIRLIN' WATERS ADVENTURE WATERPARK
(North Charleston Wannamaker County Park)

This water park features Otter Bay kiddie area, Lily Pad Lagoon toddler play area, Big Kahuna wave pool, Riptide Run mat racer slide, Tubular Twister multi-slide, Big Splash Tree House, and Rollin' River lazy river. As with all county parks, lifeguards are on duty. Gift shop, restrooms, concessions, showers/changing areas with locker rentals, and lounge chairs are all available for your use.

Admission: $19.99/General admission, $14.99/Children under 48", Children ages 2 and under are FREE, $6.99/Senior (60+), $10.99/After 3 p.m. Children ages 2 and under are FREE. Mon. – Fri. Large group rates also apply.

Hours: The waterpark opens for the summer based on the school schedule and is open only on the weekends until Jun. If you plan to visit before the first week of Jun., call ahead to check on schedule; otherwise, the waterpark is open daily from 10 a.m. – 6 p.m.

8888 University Blvd. | North Charleston
(843) 572-7275
http://www.ccprc.com/index.aspx?nid=10

FOR THE BOOKWORMS

Charleston County has over 15 libraries to choose from. Collections are extensive, including DVDs, VHS, books on CD/tape, and children's books galore, as well as an abundance activities for all ages. If you are not a resident of Charleston County, there is a $35 fee for a library card, which is valid for one year from the purchase date. I have included those branches that are closest to activities included in this guide. Summertime at the library is filled with magicians, storytellers, songs, and other special events. As of the publication date of our guide, the summer schedule was not yet available. Please check the Charleston County Public Library (CCPL) website to see what fun reading adventures await you.

Locally-owned independent bookstores are also a great place to spend time. Each location has its own specialty, but all are friendly, helpful, and filled with a diverse collection. Supporting these bookstores is the quintessential *Go Local* activity.

Public Libraries

CHARLESTON COUNTY PUBLIC LIBRARIES
www.ccpl.org

MAIN LIBRARY

Preschool Storytime (3-6 yrs) Thurs. 10 a.m.

Hours: Mon. – Thurs. 9 a.m. – 9 p.m., Fri. – Sat. 9 a.m. – 6 p.m., Sun 2 p.m. – 5 p.m.

68 Calhoun St. | Charleston
(843) 805-6930

EDISTO

Hours: Tues., Thurs. 2 p.m. – 6 p.m., Sat. 10 a.m. – 2 p.m.

1589 Hwy. 174 | Edisto Island
(843) 869-2355

FOLLY BEACH

Family Storytime (All Ages) Wed. 10 a.m.

Hours: Mon., Fri. 2 p.m. – 6 p.m., Wed. 9 a.m. – 12 p.m., Fri., Sat. 10 a.m. – 6 p.m.

55 Center St. | Folly Beach
(843) 588-2001

JAMES ISLAND

Preschool Storytime (3-6 yrs) Thurs. 10:30 a.m.

Hours: Mon. – Thurs. 10 a.m. – 8 p.m., Fri., Sat. 10 a.m. – 6 p.m.

1248 Camp Rd. | James Island
(843) 795-6679

JOHNS ISLAND

Wee Reads (Under 24 mo and Adult) Mon. 10:30 a.m.
Time for Twos (24-36 mo and Adult) Tues. 10:30 a.m.
Preschool Storytime (3-6 yrs) Wed. 10:30 a.m.
Family Storytime (All Ages) Sat. 11 a.m.

Hours: Mon. – Thurs. 10 a.m. – 8 p.m., Fri., Sat. 10 a.m. – 6 p.m.

3531 Maybank Hwy. | Johns Island
(843) 559-1945

MT. PLEASANT

Wee Reads (Under 24 mo and Adult) Tues./Thurs. 10:30 a.m.
Time for Twos (24-36 mo and Adult) Tues. 11:30 a.m./Wed. 10:30 a.m.
Preschool Storytime (3-6 yrs) Mon. 3 p.m./Wed. 11:30 a.m.
*Pre-registration requested for children's classes.

Hours: Mon. – Thurs. 10 a.m. – 8 p.m., Fri., Sat. 10 a.m. – 6 p.m.

1133 Mathis Ferry Rd. | Mt. Pleasant
(843) 849-6161

POE

Preschool Storytime (3-6 yrs) Tues. 10:30 a.m., Thurs. 10:15 a.m.

Hours: Mon., Fri. 2 p.m. – 6 p.m., Tues., Thurs., Sat. 10 a.m. – 2 p.m.

1921 I'on Ave. | Sullivan's Island
(843) 883-3914

ST. ANDREWS

Wee Reads (Under 24 mo and Adult) Wed./Thurs. 10:30 a.m.
Time for Twos (24-36 mo and Adult) Tues. 10:30 a.m./Thurs. 11:30 a.m.
Preschool Storytime (3-6 yrs) Tues./Wed. 11:30 a.m.

Hours: Mon. – Thurs. 10 a.m. – 8 p.m., Fri., Sat. 10 a.m. – 6 p.m.

1735 N. Woodmere Dr. | West Ashley
(843) 766-2546

VILLAGE

Hours: Mon., Fri. 10 a.m. – 6 p.m., Tues., Thurs. 2 p.m. – 6 p.m., Sat. 10 a.m. – 2 p.m.

430 Whilden St. | Mt. Pleasant
(843) 884-9741

Independently Owned Book Stores

BLUE BICYCLE BOOKS

Blue Bicycle has been voted the best book store in Charleston for 5 years in a row. It's a landmark to the locals. With over 50,000 volumes, the selections consist of history, architecture, Civil War, religion, philosophy, gardening, classics, poetry, science, and fiction. The store specializes in used, rare, and local books.

Hours: Mon. – Wed. 10 a.m. – 6 p.m., Thurs. - Sat. 10 a.m. - 7:30 p.m., Sun. 1 p.m. – 6 p.m.

420 King St. | Charleston
(843) 722-2666
info@bluebicyclebooks.com

BOOK EXCHANGE

If you have enough time to relax and finish a book on vacation and are anxious to start the next, the Book Exchange is the place for you. Bring your mass-market audio books, children's books, and paperbacks to the store for a credit for a future purchase. If you don't have books to exchange, you can still make a selection from the volumes in the stacks.

Hours: Mon. – Fri. 10 a.m. – 8 p.m., Sat. 10 a.m. – 6 p.m.

1131 Savannah Hwy. | West Ashley
(843) 556-5051

INDIGO BOOKS

Indigo Books is a locally owned and independent bookstore located on the main street of Freshfields Village, just outside of Kiawah Island. One-on-one attention from the store employees and the owners, combined with the many nooks and crannies of local-interest books and national sellers, give the visitor a cozy feeling. In addition to books, Indigo Books sells cards, stationery, and a few small book-related toys for children. If you are looking for a title not in Indigo's stacks, the owners offer to order it for you for a later pickup. Next door is a small coffee shop café where you can sit, enjoy a cup of coffee, and dive into your newest novel or travel guide!

Hours: Mon. – Sat. 10 a.m. – 5 p.m., Sun. 1 p.m. – 5 p.m.

472 Freshfields Dr. | Johns Island
(843) 768-2275 or (888) 825-9264

RAVENOUS READER

Despite its small size, Ravenous Reader has a wonderful selection of books. The owner usually carries one copy of most titles, but the store will be glad to special-order any book if you have something in mind. The café provides coffee and tea for you to sip while perusing the pages of your new acquisition.

Hours: Mon. – Fri. 10 a.m. – 7 p.m., Sat. 10 a.m. – 5 p.m.

792 Folly Rd # E | James Island
(843) 795-2700

SULLIVAN'S TRADE A BOOK

Looking for another way to go green and trade in your well-taken-care-of books? Go no further. Bring in your paperbacks and audio books for trade at Sullivan's Trade A Book. Books can also be purchased without a book to trade.

Hours: Mon. – Fri. 10 a.m. – 6:30 p.m., Sat. 10 a.m. – 6 p.m.

1303 Ben Sawyer Blvd., Ste 3 | Mt. Pleasant
(843) 884-8611

Playing Around

Charleston has its share of indoor play places, amusement parks, bowling lanes, ice skating and roller skating rinks, as well as the ever-popular jump castles. Most of these locations are on the outskirts of town and away from the average visitor's path. The locations listed here are those that come recommended from parents with kids of all ages.

Sporting pastimes are a wonderful way to spend quality time with the entire family. Charleston has three teams: Charleston Battery Soccer, Riverdogs Baseball, and Stingrays Ice Hockey (yes, ice hockey). So head out to the games, eat a loaded hotdog and twisty pretzel, wash it down with a soft drink, and root, root, root for the home team!

Bowling

AMF CHARLESTON LANES

Hours: Mon. - Thurs. 9 a.m. – 12 a.m., Fri. 9 a.m. – 1 a.m., Sat. 9 a.m. – 2 a.m., Sun. 10 a.m. – 12 a.m.

1963 Savannah Hwy. | West Ashley
(843) 766-0241
www.amf.com/charleston

ASHLEY LANES

Hours: Mon. 9 a.m. – 1 a.m., Tues. 9 a.m. – 9 p.m., Wed. 12 p.m. – 11 p.m., Thurs. 9 a.m. - 11 p.m., Fri. 10 a.m. – 1a.m., Sat. 9 a.m. – 2 a.m., Sun. 12 p.m. – 11 p.m.

1568 Sam Rittenberg Blvd. | West Ashley
(843) 766-9061

TWIN RIVER LANES

Hours: Mon. – Sat. 8 a.m. – 2 a.m., Sun. 8 a.m. – Midnight.

613 Johnnie Dodds Blvd. | Mt. Pleasant
(843) 884-7735

Skating Rinks

CAROLINA ICE PALACE

Hours and rates vary seasonally. When special events are planned, public admission hours change to accommodate visitors. Please call ahead of time to ensure the rink is open and to check on any admission fee specials or changes.

Admission: $7/Adult, $6/Senior, $6/Child (4 – 12), $3/Children under 4. Skate Rental: $3

Hours: Mon. 9 a.m. – 5:30 p.m., Wed. 9 a.m. – 9 p.m., Fr.i 9 a.m. – 10 p.m., Sat. 12:30 p.m. – 10 p.m., Sun. 1:30 p.m. – 6 p.m. Closed to public skating Tues. and Thurs., but open for private groups.

7665 Northwoods Blvd. | North Charleston
(843) 572-2717
www.carolinaicepalace.com

HOT WHEELS SKATE CENTER

Admission: Wed. $3, Thurs. $3, Fri. $8, Sat. (Youth Skate) $4 and adults skate FREE with paid child, Sat. (All Ages) $5, Sat. (7 – 10 p.m.) $6, Sun. (Family Skate) $4. Sessions include regular quad rental skates. Speed rentals available for $3.

Hours: Wed. 3:30 p.m. – 5 p.m.; Thurs. 7 – 9 p.m. (18 and over), Fri. 7 p.m. – 11 p.m. (all ages), Sat. 11 a.m. – 1 p.m. (11 and under), 2 p.m. – 5 p.m. (all ages), 7 p.m. – 10 p.m., Sun. 2 p.m. – 5 p.m. (family skate all ages).

1523 Folly Rd. | James Island
(843) 795-7982
www.hotwheelsskating.net

Bounce Houses

Both indoor recreation areas offer 12,000 square feet of inflatable fun. Kids of all ages enjoy bouncing, so plan to spend a good deal of time here. Remember those socks, as they must be worn at all times. Children must be accompanied by an adult at all times. A food menu is available for on-site snacking.

EAST SHORE ATHLETIC CLUB FUN FIT!

Mom's Morning Out: Walkers – five years old can spend Friday mornings from 10 a.m. – 12:30 p.m. under the watchful eye of staff members. Lunch is provided for an additional $5. Cost $30/Day.

Teen Night: A safe place to turn your teens loose for three hours on a Saturday night for $10? Yes, it's true. For teens aged 12 – 17 yrs. Drop them off from 7 – 10 p.m. the 1st Saturday night of each month.

Open Jump is available daily without reservations or time limitations; however, call on the weekends to make sure that no parties are scheduled which affect jump times.

Admission: $5/4 yrs. and under, $7/4+, $10/Any child on Sat. and Sun.

Hours: Mon. – Fri. 10 a.m. – 6 p.m., Sat. – call before arriving, Sun. 2 – 5 p.m.

2300 Clements Ferry Rd., Ste 204 | Daniel Island
(843) 971-8109
www.ready-set-jump.com

JUMP INDOORS OF CHARLESTON

Open Jump is available daily. There is also an arcade and small child area (ages four and under) on site when the kids need a break from the bouncing.

Admission: $6/1-hr., $9/2-hrs., $19/Full day. "Bounce Club Card" would pay off if you plan on staying in town for a week: one week of unlimited bouncing $25/Pass.

Hours: Mon. – Sat. 10 a.m. – 7 p.m., Sun. 1– 7 p.m.

5101 Ashley Phosphate Rd. Ste. 149 | North Charleston
(Behind Bank of America)
(843) 767-3979
www.jumpindoors.com

Amusement Parks and Mini Golf

FRANKIE'S FUN HOUSE

Frankie's Fun House allows kids to cut loose and drive cars around a course, play mini golf, drop coins in arcade games, play bumper boats, and rock climb, all in one place.

Admission: There is no set admission fee. Fees are based on activity.

Hours: Mon. – Sat. 10 a.m. – midnight, Sun. 12 p.m. – 12 a.m. Some activities open later in the day than others, so call in advance if you want details.

5000 Ashley Phosphate Rd. | North Charleston
(843) 767-1376
www.frankiesfunpark.com

BLACKBEARD'S COVE FAMILY FUN PARK

Located in Mt. Pleasant three miles north of the Isle of Palms Connector, this park is a bit of a drive, but if you are looking for a way to fill the better part of a day or an activity to round out a day trip from the northern reaches of the county, this is the place. Activities include go-carts, climbing wall, jump land, all day indoor play system, water wars, mini golf, laser tag, arcade, and Blackbeard's Gemstone Mining. Food is available on site.

Admission: There is no admission fee. Fees are based on activity. Packages (mini golf and activity choices) range from $11.95 - $19.95. Individual activities range from $5.00 - $13.95, with laser tag being the most expensive.

Hours: Mon. – Sat. 10 – 12 a.m., Sun. 12 – 11 p.m. Call in advance of your trip to confirm, as seasonal hours vary.

3255 Hwy. 17 North | Mt. Pleasant
(843) 971-1223
www.blackbeardscove.net

CLASSIC GOLF

1528 Ben Sawyer Blvd. | Mt. Pleasant
(843) 881-3131

Sports Teams

For the small city that Charleston still is, we have quite the selection of professional sports to choose from. Game nights are terrifically family friendly. In fact, there are usually theme nights and other children's play areas which make an already fun sporting event livelier. Check the team website or call for seasonal schedule. Parking is extra, so bring cash.

SOUTH CAROLINA STINGRAYS HOCKEY

Tickets: You may purchase tickets on-site or in advance via Ticketmaster (www.ticketmaster.com). Seating prices for 2010: Riser $21, Lower Level $18, Upper Level $15. Discount of $1 applies for an advance purchase.

Directions: Take I-26 West to Exit 213/Montague Ave and turn left. Follow Montague past International Blvd. and you'll see the Coliseum on your right.

North Charleston Coliseum
5001 Coliseum Dr. | North Charleston
(843) 744-2248
www.stingrayshockey.com

CHARLESTON BATTERY MAJOR LEAGUE SOCCER

Tickets: Purchase tickets online, call the ticket hotline, or walk up to the gate. Regular season seating prices for 2010 are as follows: West Stand/ Club Seat $15, West Stand/Bleacher $10, East Stand/Box $12, East Stand/ Bleacher $8, General Admission $10. If you don't mind shelling out a few extra bucks, sit in the West Stands so the sun (in all its glory) won't pierce your pupils before it sets.

Directions: Take Hwy. 17 North to Mt. Pleasant. Travel through Mt. Pleasant, then take I-526 towards North Charleston. Take Exit 24 onto Daniel Island and merge onto Seven Farms Road. Drive through the center of Daniel Island and make a right onto Daniel Island Drive. Blackbaud Stadium is on the right.

Blackbaud Stadium
1990 Daniel Island Dr. | Daniel Island
(843) 971-GOAL (ticket hotline)
www.charlestonbattery.com

CHARLESTON RIVERDOGS MINOR LEAGUE BASEBALL

Tickets: Purchase tickets online, call the box office, or walk up to the gate. Ticket prices for the 2010 season are as follows: Children 3 and under are FREE without a seat, Box Seats $12, Lower Reserve $8, Upper Reserve $7, General Admission $5.

Directions: Take Meeting Street to Spring Street until it turns into Lockwood Dr. Turn right on Lockwood Dr., and the stadium is on the left.

"The Joe" Stadium
360 Fishburne St. | Charleston
(843) 577-3647 (box office)
www.riverdogs.com

Handy Phone Numbers and Information

Emergency Numbers

Emergency (Police, Fire, and Ambulance)	911
Poison Control Hotline	(800) 222-1222
Crime Stoppers	(843) 554-1111
Greater Charleston Emergency Vet Clinic	(843) 744-3372
TTY Emergency Help for Customers with Disabilities	(843) 744-3200
Wildlife Law Enforcement	(800) 922-5431
Animal Control	(843) 202-1700
Charleston County Emergency Preparedness	(843) 202-7400

Area Hospitals

East Cooper Regional Medical Center – Mt. Pleasant	(843) 881-0100
Bon Secours – St. Francis Hospital - West Ashley	(843) 402-1000
Charleston Memorial Hospital – Charleston	(843) 577-0600
Medical University of SC Medical Center – Charleston	(843) 792-2300
Roper Hospital – Charleston	(843) 724-2000
Trident Medical Center – North Charleston	(843) 797-7000

Driving Distances

All points listed are based on travel time in miles from the City of Charleston Visitor's Center at 375 Meeting Street to the main entrance of the destination town.

Awendaw	24
Daniel Island	16
Edisto Beach	47
Folly Beach	20
Goose Creek	9
Hollywood	18
Isle of Palms	12
Johns Island	8
Kiawah Island	22
McClellanville	38
Mt. Pleasant	5
Moncks Corner	30
Ravenel	18
Sullivan's Island	9
Summerville	25
Wadmalaw Island	12
West Ashley (Hwy. 17/61 split)	4

Getting Around - Driving, Parking, and Peddling About

Charleston is very accessible by car. That being said, the streets through downtown can get very crowded with sightseeing cars, horse-drawn carriages, students, locals, and tourists. Bus lines, taxis, pedicabs, bikes, and a strong set of legs will get you just about anywhere in the area. If you do choose to drive, you'll find that street parking in downtown Charleston is difficult to locate, so utilize one of the city's many parking garages. Renting a bike is another great way to sightsee and get around.

CHARLESTON AREA TRANSPORTATION AUTHORITY (CARTA)

CARTA offers connecting routes on the Charleston peninsula, to area beaches, and to major shopping and attractions. The system is very much a work in progress, and it does work best if you have a flexible schedule. Buses are bike friendly, but you must leave the pets behind.

Rates: $1.50/Adult, 75¢/Senior aged 55+ (with ID). Children under 6 ride FREE. The following passes are also available: $5/All day; $11/3-days; $12/10-trips; $37.50/31-days; $42/40-trips. Passes apply to Downtown Area Shuttles as well as Fixed Route Service.

36 John St. | Charleston
(843) 724-7240
www.ridecarta.com

CHARLESTON BLACK CAB COMPANY varies

Charleston Black Cab Company is known for its London-style taxis. Riders may call in advance for a taxi between 6 a.m. – 3 a.m. The area is broken into zones, and rates are based on travel within or between those zones, with downtown Charleston as the base. These taxis will get you anywhere you need to go in Charleston County.

PO Box 22207 | Charleston
(843) 216-2627
www.charlestonblackcabcompany.com

CHARLESTON GREEN TAXI varies

Charleston Green Taxi touts a fleet of hybrid vehicles offering green travel throughout the area. Rates are based on the destination zone. Reservations can be made in advance. Charleston does not have taxis roaming the street waiting to be hailed, so for the most part, you will need to call to get a ride.

334 East Bay Street | Charleston
(843) 819-0846
www.charlestongreentaxi.com

CHARLESTON WATER TAXI

If you are looking to head back and forth from the Charleston Peninsula to Mt. Pleasant, the water taxi is your ticket. The ride takes about an hour, and the scenery is beautiful. Bikes and pets are allowed.

Rates: $5/Adult (one way), $8/Adult (round trip), $12/Adult (all day), Children under 5 are FREE.

Charleston Maritime Center
Concord St. | Charleston

Charleston Harbor Resort
Patriot's Point Rd. | Mt. Pleasant
(843) 330-2989
www.charlestonwatertaxi.com

Pedicabs and Rickshaws

If you are looking for a super cool and unusual way to see the city while en route to your next destination, pedicabs and rickshaws are the way to go. The "cab" is open, as though you are a in a Roman Chariot (the upside is you get to sit down). Your driver peddles furiously while spouting occasional tidbits about the town. The kids will surely love this, probably almost as much as you will.

CHARLESTON BIKE TAXI

Charleston Bike Taxi is available to pick you up seven days a week. You'll see these bikers riding about the streets and can often hail them instead of calling.

Rates: $4.50/Person, per 10 minutes. Drivers can get 2 people just about anywhere downtown in 10 minutes or less.

Hours: Sun. - Tues. 10 a.m. – 11 p.m., Wed. and Thurs. 10:30 a.m. – 1 a.m., Fri. and Sat. 10:30 a.m. - 2:30 a.m.

(843) 532-8663
www.biketaxi.net

CHARLESTON RICKSHAW

Available seven days a week from 9 a.m. – 2 a.m. You may call ahead to reserve your space or hail one if you see it riding around.

Rates: $4.50/Person, per 10 minute ride.

(843) 723-5685
www.charlestonrickshaw.com

2010 Special Events Calendar

Go Local Charleston has covered the many daily and ongoing events available at each of our exciting destinations, however there are many more activities that occur only during certain times of the year that are worth checking out. The following list should keep you more than busy, but should you crave more the Charleston Area Visitors and Convention Bureau has an extensive calendar on their site: www.charlestoncvb.com. If you would like admission prices, hours or more details about a particular event please contact the host venue or visit their website.

January

11/13/2009 – 1/3 Festival of Lights | James Island County Park
www.ccprc.com   (843) 795-4FUN

1/1 New Year's Day Parade | Charleston
www.charlestoncity.info   (843) 571-4061

1/9 The Charleston Museum's Oyster Roast | James Island
www.charlestonmuseum.org   (843) 722-2996

1/9 – 1/10 The Wizard of Oz | North Charleston Performing Arts Center
www.colisumpac.com   (843) 529-5000 ext. 5113

1/29 – 1/30 Charleston Youth Co Winter Spectacular | Sottile Theatre
www.charlestonyouthcompany.com   (843) 693-6664

1/31 27th Annual Lowcountry Oyster Festival | Boone Hall Plantation
www.charlestonrestaurantassociation.com   (843) 364-0971

February

2/1 – 2/28 Black History Month – Charleston County Public Libraries

2/4 – 2/6 Robert Ivey Ballet – The Velveteen Rabbit | Sottile Theatre
www.robertiveyballet.com   (843) 556-1343

2/6 Chamber Music Charleston Classical Kids: Mercedes and the
Chocolate Pilot | Circular Congregational Church
www.chambermusiccharleston.org/classicalkids   (843) 763-4941

2/12-2/14 Southeastern Wildlife Exposition | Charleston
www.sewe.com   (843) 723-1748

2/20 Fossil Festival | Cypress Gardens
www.cypressgardens.info   (843) 553-0515

2/20-2/12 Civil War Encamp.m.ent | Middleton Place
www.middletonplace.org   (843) 556-6020

March

3/1 – 3/31 Women's History Month – Special Events at all Library
Branches

3/1 Read Across America | Charleston County Public Libraries
www.ccpl.org   (843) 805-6930

3/6-3/7 Flower and Art Show | Cypress Gardens
www.cypressgardens.info   (843) 553-0515

3/6 - 3/24 Charleston Ballet Theatre – Pinocchio | Sottile Theatre
www.charlestonballet.org   (843) 723-7334

3/10-3/14 Ferdinand the Bull | Sottile Theatre
www.charlestonstage.com   (843) 577-7183

3/12 – 3/14 A Year with Frog and Toad | Sottile Theatre
www.charlestonstage.com   (843) 577-5967

3/17 Charleston's Annual St. Patrick's Day Celebration | Charleston
www.charlestoncity.info   (843) 556-3578

3/17 Catch the Leprechaun Race | Patriots Point
www.patriotspoint.org   (843) 884-2727

3/26-3/28 YMCA Flowertown Festival | Summerville
www.summervilleymca.org   (843) 871-9622

3/26-3/27 Breath of Spring Music Festival | Cypress Gardens
www.cypressgardens.info   (843) 553-0515

3/27 Cooper River Bridge Run | Mount Pleasant
www.bridgerun.com   (843) 856-1949

3/26 Cooper River "The Kids Run" | Charleston
www.bridgerun.com   (843) 856-1949

April

Apr-December - The Civil War Sesquicentennial (The Ft. Sumter – Ft. Moultrie Historical Trust)

4/3 Easter Eggstravanza | Middleton Place
www.middletonplace.org   (843) 556-6020

4/3 Edisto Art Guild Spring Show and Sale | Edisto Island
www.edistochamber.com   (843) 869-3867

4/16-4/19 Battle of Charleston at Legare Farms | Johns Island
www.legarefarms.com   (843) 559-0763

4/16 - 4/18 East Coast Canoe & Kayak Festival | James Island Cnty. Park
www.ccprc.com

4/16 Earth Day Festival | North Charleston
www.charlestoncounty.org
(843) 720-7111

4/17 - 4/18 Lowcountry Strawberry Festival | Boone Hall
www.boonehallplantation.com   (843) 884-4371

4/22-4/25 Winnie the Pooh | Sottile Theatre
www.charlestonstage.com   (843) 577-7183

4/24 Chamber Music Charleston – Classical Kids Series: Peter and the
Wolf | Circular Congregational Church
www.chambermusiccharleston.org/classicalkids   (843) 763-4941

4/25 22nd Annual Blessing of the Fleet and Seafood Festival | Mt.
Pleasant
www.townofmountpleasant.com   (843) 884-8517 ext. 3402

4/24-4/25 Sheep and Wool Days | Middleton Place
www.middletonplace.org   (843) 556-6020

4/24 Edisto Island Community Parade | Edisto Island
www.edistochamber.com   (843) 869-3867

4/30 – 5/8 North Charleston Arts Festival | North Charleston
www.northcharleston.org   (843) 740-5854

May

5/1 Edisto Day Bazaar Arts and Crafts Festival | Edisto Island
www.edistochamber.com   (843) 869-3867

5/18- 6/2 Interactive Rice Planting and Cultivation | Middleton Place
www.middletonplace.org   (843) 556-6020

5/28-6/13 Spoleto/Piccolo Spoleto | Charleston Area
www.piccolospoleto.com   www.spoletousa.org

5/31 Memorial Day Ceremony | Patriots Point
www.patriotspoint.org   (843) 884-2727

June

5/18- 6/2 Interactive Rice Planting and Cultivation | Middleton Place
www.middletonplace.org   (843) 556-6020

5/28-6/13 Spoleto/Piccolo Spoleto | Charleston Area
www.piccolospoleto.com   www.spoletousa.org

6/5 Annual Sweetgrass Cultural Arts Festival | Mount Pleasant
www.sweetgrassfestival.org   (843) 856-9732

6/5 Sand Sculpting Contest | Isle of Palms
www.iop.net   (843) 886-6428

6/5 Lowcountry Splash | Patriots Point
www.patriotspoint.org   (843) 884-2727

6/6 Spoleto Finale | Middleton Place
www.middletonplace.org   (843) 556-6020

6/18-6/20 Selu and Anikituhwa Indian Crafts Festival | Patriots Point
www.patriotspoint.org   (843) 884-2727

6/18-6/20 Charleston Harbor Fest | Charleston Maritime Center
www.charlestonharborfest.org   (843) 722-1030

July

7/2-7/4 Independence Day | Middleton Place
www.middletonplace.org   (843) 556-6020

7/4 July 4th Festival | Cypress Gardens
www.cypressgardens.info   (843) 553-0515

7/4 4th of July Blast | Patriots Point
www.patriotspoint.org   (843) 884-2727

7/11 – 11/28 (Saturdays only) Pirate Play | Charleston Powder Magazine
www.powdermag.org   (843) 722-9350

August

8/15 Summerville Family YMCA – Y-Tri Youth Triathalon | Summerville
www.summervilleymca.org   (843) 871-9622

September

9/1 – 9/30 Hispanic Heritage Month – Charleston County Public Libraries

9/5 Bluegrass Festival | Boone Hall Plantation
www.boonehallplantation.com   (843) 884-4371

9/11 Patriot Day Remembrance Ceremony | Patriots Point
www.patriotspoint.org   (843) 884-2727

9/18, 9/21, 9/29 Interactive Rice Harvest | Middleton Place
www.middletonplace.org   (843) 556-6020

9/23-10/3 MOJA Arts Festival: A Celebration of African-American and
Caribbean Arts |Charleston
www.mojafestival.com   (800) 745-3000

9/16 Scottish Games and Highland Gathering | Boone Hall Plantation
www.boonehallplantation.com   (843) 216-1032

9/26 Charleston Green Fair | Charleston
www.charlestongreenfair.com   (843) 513-2655

9/26 Smithsonian Museum Day | Participating Charleston Museums
http://microsite.smithsonianmag.com/museumday

October

9/23-10/3 MOJA Arts Festival: A Celebration of African-American and
Caribbean Arts | Charleston
www.mojafestival.com   (800) 745-3000

10/1 - 10/31 Pumpkin Patch & Fright Nights | Boone Hall Plantation
www.boonehallplantation.com   (843) 884-4371

10/2 – 11/1 West Farm Corn Maze | Monks Corner
www.westfarmcornmaze.com   (843) 408-2284

10/9 Edisto Art Guild Fall Show and Sale | Edisto Island
www.edistochamber.com   (843) 869-3867

10/16 Edisto Fall Festival | Edisto Island
www.edistochamber.com   (843) 869-3867

10/16 - 10/17 Plantation Days | Middleton Place
www.middletonplace.org   (843) 556-6020

10/17 Mt. Pleasant Children's Day Festival | Mt. Pleasant
www.townofmountpleasant.com   (843) 884-8517 ext. 3402

10/23 - 10/24 Halloween in the Swamp | Cypress Gardens
www.cypressgardens.info   (843) 553-0515

10/28 – 11/8 Coastal Carolina Fair | Ladson
www.coastalcarolinafair.org

November

10/28 – 11/8 Coastal Carolina Fair | Ladson
www.coastalcarolinafair.org

10/2 – 11/1 West Farm Corn Maze | Monks Corner
www.westfarmcornmaze.com   (843) 408-2284

11/6 Harvest Festival at Mullet Hall Equestrian Center | Johns Island
www.ccprc.com   (843) 795-4FUN

11/11 - 11/14 Veterans Day Week | Patriot's Point
www.patriotspoint.org   (843) 884-2727

11/12 – 1/2 Holiday Festival of Lights | James Island County Park
www.ccprc.com   (843) 795-4FUN

11/13 - 11/14 Plantation Days | Middleton Place
www.middletonplace.org   (843) 556-6020

11/13 - 11/14 Battle of Secessionville | Boone Hall Plantation
www.boonehallplantation.com   (843) 884-4371

11/25 Turkey Day Run and Gobble Wobble 5k | Charleston
www.turkeydayrun.com

December

11/12 – 1/2 Holiday Festival of Lights | James Island County Park
www.ccprc.com   (843) 795-4FUN

12/4 Reindeer Run 5k | Charleston
www.reindeerrun.org

12/4 City of Charleston Official Tree Lighting Ceremony and Parade of
Boats | Charleston
www.charlestonarts.sc   (843) 724-7414

12/5 Mt. Pleasant Tree Lighting Ceremony | Mt. Pleasant
www.townofmountpleasant.com   (843) 884-8517 ext. 3402

12/11 Family Yuletide | Middleton Place
www.middletonplace.org   (843) 556-6020

12/11 19th Annual Edisto Beach Christmas & Boat Parade | Edisto Beach
www.edistochamber.com   (843) 869-3867

12/12 Mt. Pleasant Christmas Parades | Mt. Pleasant
www.townofmountpleasant.com   (843) 884-8517 ext. 3402

12/12 Edisto Community Chorus Christmas Concert | Edisto Beach
www.edistochamber.com   (843) 869-3867

12/17 - 12/18 Middleton Place Grand Illumination | Middleton Place
www.middletonplace.org   (843) 556-6020

12/18 Santa in the South | Cypress Gardens
www.cypressgardens.info   (843) 553-0515

12/19 Summerville Christmas Parade | Summerville
www.summervilledream.org   (843) 821-7260

12/31 Happy New Year Charleston | Charleston
www.charlestonarts.sc   (843) 724-7308

South Carolina Produce Availability

The following chart summarizes the produce availability across the state. Most farmer's markets allow growers from around the state to participate, so there's a good chance you will see these varieties when shopping around. Weather greatly affects when crops can be harvested, so remember this is a loose schedule - Mother Nature can be fickle.

January: Beets, Cilantro, Leeks, Mixed Leafy Greens.

February: Beets, Cilantro, Green Onions, Leeks, Mixed Leafy Greens, Parsley, Radishes.

March: Asparagus, Beets, Cilantro, Green Onions, Leeks, Mixed Leafy Greens, Oriental Vegetables, Parsley, Radishes, Strawberries.

April: Asparagus, Beets, Cabbage, Cilantro, Green Onions, Leeks, Mixed Leafy Greens, Oriental Vegetables, Parsley, Radishes, Strawberries.

May: Asparagus, Beans, Beets, Broccoli, Cabbage, Cilantro, Cucumbers, Green Onions, Leeks, Mixed Leafy Greens, Oriental Vegetables, Parsley, Peaches, Peas, Radishes, Strawberries, Squash, Sweet Corn.

June: Beans, Beets, Blackberries, Blueberries, Broccoli, Cabbage, Cantaloupes, Cilantro, Cucumbers, Green Onions, Leeks, Mixed Leafy Greens, Oriental Vegetables, Parsley, Peaches, Peas, Peppers, Radishes, Strawberries, Squash, Sweet Corn, Tomatoes, Watermelons.

July: Beans, Beets, Blackberries, Blueberries, Broccoli, Butter Beans, Cantaloupes, Cilantro, Green Onions, Leeks, Mixed Leafy Greens, Okra, Parsley, Peaches, Peanuts (Green), Peas, Peppers, Radishes, Squash, Sweet Corn, Tomatoes, Watermelons.

August: Beans, Beets, Butter Beans, Cantaloupes, Cilantro, Green Onions, Leeks, Mixed Leafy Greens, Okra, Parsley, Peaches, Peanuts (Green), Peas, Peppers, Squash, Sweet Corn, Sweet Potatoes.

September: Apples, Beans, Beets, Butter Beans, Cilantro, Green Onions, Leeks, Mixed Leafy Greens, Muscadine Grapes, Okra, Oriental Vegetables, Parsley, Peaches, Peanuts (Green), Peas, Peppers, Radishes, Squash, Sweet Potatoes, Watermelon.

October: Apples, Beans, Beets, Broccoli, Butter Beans, Cilantro, Cucumbers, Green Onions, Leeks, Mixed Leafy Greens, Muscadine Grapes, Okra, Oriental Vegetables, Parsley, Peas, Pecans, Peppers, Radishes, Squash, Sweet Potatoes, Watermelon.

November: Apples, Beets, Broccoli, Butter Beans, Cilantro, Green Onions, Leeks, Mixed Leafy Greens, Muscadine Grapes, Parsley, Peas, Pecans, Peppers, Radishes, Sweet Potatoes.

December: Apples, Beets, Broccoli, Cilantro, Leeks, Mixed Leafy Greens, Parsley, Pecans, Radishes, Sweet Potatoes.

Source: www.usda.gov

Index By Location

Awendaw, 37, 47, 65, 87, 96, 103
Charleston, 46, 49, 50, 51, 53, 59,
    63, 67, 70, 73, 74, 80, 81, 92,
    93, 96, 104, 106, 107, 108, 128,
    129, 131, 146, 149, 154, 160,
    161, 163, 164, 165, 166
Cottageville, 35
Daniel Island, 42, 109, 129, 156,
    160
Edisto Beach, 95, 104, 134
Edisto Island, 39, 124, 134, 146
Folly Beach, 47, 51, 52, 53, 55,
    57, 129, 131, 135, 136, 137,
    146, 162
Greenpond, 87, 91
Hollywood, 52, 92, 95, 128
Isle of Palms, 47, 52, 53, 58, 74,
    75, 76, 78, 87, 93, 110, 131,
    137, 138, 139, 140, 158, 171
James Island, 55, 67, 69, 94, 104,
    110, 111, 131, 135, 142, 147,
    150
Johns Island, 40, 56, 57, 58, 64,
    72, 94, 111, 112, 122, 124, 125,
    126, 127, 129, 130, 131, 139,
    140, 147, 150
Kiawah Island, 51, 71, 138, 140,
    135, 150
McClellanville, 102, 112, 130

Mt. Pleasant, 19, 23, 37, 47, 48,
    50, 52, 54, 55, 59, 60, 69, 73,
    74, 90, 93, 113, 114, 115, 123,
    129, 130, 131, 138, 141, 147,
    148, 154, 158, 160, 161, 165
Moncks Corner, 13, 16
North Charleston, 26, 27, 61, 70,
    116, 117, 130, 142, 143, 154,
    157, 159, 160, 161
Ravenel, 36, 62, 105, 123, 138,
    141
Ridgeville, 100
Shem Creek, 47, 48, 90, 93, 131
Sullivan's Island, 18, 19, 55, 74,
    93, 117, 140, 141, 148
Summerville, 15, 65, 103, 118,
    125, 130
Wadmalaw Island, 46, 47, 57, 77,
    122, 130
West Ashley, 14, 38, 59, 71, 92,
    93, 118, 119, 135, 136, 137,
    139, 148, 149, 154, 161

Index By Attraction

Ackerman Park, 59
AIR, 53
Alhambra Hall, 113
Ambrose Family Farm, 122, 123
AMF Charleston Lanes, 154
Angel Oak, 111, 112
Aquarium Wharf, 41, 81
Ashley Lanes, 154
Audubon Swamp at Frances
Beidler Forest, 85
Awendaw Passage of the
Palmetto Trail, 96
Backman Seafood, 130
Barrier Island Eco Tours, 48, 75
Beachwalker Park, 71, 127, 133,
135, 138
Bear Island WMA, 86
Bee City Honey Bee Farm and
Petting Zoo, 34
Blackbeard's Cove Family Fun
Park, 158
Blue Bicycle Books, 149
Bohicket Boat Adventure & Tour
Company, 46, 76
Bohicket Creek Boat Rentals, 77
Book Exchange, 149
Boone Hall Farm, 122
Boone Hall Market Store and
Market Café, 123
Boone Hall Plantation, 12
Brittlebank Park, 106
Buck Hall Recreation Area
Trailhead, 96, 97
Bull Dog Tours, 27
Cape Romain NWR, 87, 88, 103

Capers Island Heritage Preserve,
75, 78, 87
Captain Hatt's Shrimp Market,
130
Carolina Ice Palace, 155
Caw Caw Interpretive Center, 35,
105, 135
Center for Birds of Prey, 35, 36
Champney's Blueberry Farm, 122
Charles Towne Landing, 33, 35,
37, 87, 104
Charlesotn Riverdogs MLB, 160
Charleston Battery MLS, 159
Charleston Bicycle Company, 70
Charleston County Public
Libraries, 146-148
Charleston Area Farmer's
Markets, 121, 124, 128-130
Charleston Watersport
Outfitters, 54
Charleston's Museum Mile, 11,
17, 20, 23, 24
Charlotte Street Park, 107
Cherry Point Seafood, 130
Children's Museum of the
Lowcountry, 13, 17
Classic Golf, 158
Coastal Eco Tours, 78
Coastal Expeditions, 47, 89
Crab Bank Seabird Sanctuary, 90
Crosby's on Folly, 131
Crosby's Seafood, 131
Cypress Gardens, 13
Donnely WMA, 90

Dungannon Heritage Preserve, 91
Earnest F. Hollings ACE Basin NWR, 94
Earth Fare, 131
East Coast Greenway, 92
East Shore Athletic Club Fun Fit, 156
Edisto Beach State Park, 104, 134
Edisto Island Serpentarium, 39, 134
Enchanted Acres Equestrian Center, 65
Etiwan Park, 109
Folly Beach, 52, 57, 135, 146
Folly Beach County Park, 136
Folly Beach Fishing Pier, 136
Folly Beach Watersports, 55
Fort Moultrie, 18-20
Fort Sumter, 18-20, 108
Fox Farms, 62
Francis Marion National Forest, 96-99, 103
Frankie's Fun House, 157
Freshfields Village, 129, 139, 150
Gahagan Park, 118
Gibbes Museum of Art, 20
Givhans Ferry State Park, 100
Greenhill Community Center, 113
H2Osmosis Sports & H2Oz Training Center, 56
Half-Moon Outfitters, 66
Hampton Park & McMahon Playground, 106
Harborview/Ft. Johnson Park, 110
Hazel Parker Playground, 107

Hot Wheels Skate Center, 155
I'on Swamp Interpretive Trail, 97
Indigo Books, 150
Island Bike & Surf Shop, 57, 71
Island Breeze Tours, 79
Isle of Palms County Park, 138
Isle of Palms Recreation Department, 110
James Island County Park, 48, 67, 110, 142
Jeremiah Farm and Goat Dairy, 40
Johns Island Park, 112
Joseph Field's Farm, 124
Jump Indoors of Charleston,
Kayak Charleston
King's Market, 124
Legare Farms, 125
Liberty Square, 19
Magnolia Plantation and Gardens, 14, 87, 105
Mary Utsey Playground, 118
Middleton Place, 14, 50
Middleton Place Equestrian Center, 63
Middleton Place Outdoor Center, 49
Mike's Bikes, 72
Moultrie Playground, 107
Mount Pleasant Skate Park, 60
Mt. Pleasant Pier, 114
Mt. Pleasant Seafood, 131
Myers Blueberries, 125
Nature Adventures & Canoe Outfitters, Inc., 50
North Charleston Park Circle, 116

Old Charleston Tours, 28
Old Exchange and Provost Dungeon, 13, 21, 22, 29, 108
Old Santee Canal Park, 15
Oli Nah (Floyd's), 58
Paddlefish Kayaking, 51
Paintball Charleston, 70
Palmetto Islands County Park, 104, 113, 141
Palmetto Surfer's Blog, 58
Park West Complex, 114
Patriots Point Naval and Maritime Museum, 13, 19, 23, 93
Plymouth Park, 111
Powder Magazine, 23
Raul's Seafood Market, 131
Ravenous Reader, 150
Rein and Shine Therapeutic Riding, 65
Remley's Point Community Center, 115
Richard L. Jones Center, 115
Riverfront Park, 117,
Riverlanding Children's Park, 109
Robert E. Ashley Landing, 112
Rosebank Farms, 127
Sandlapper Water Tours, 80
Santee Coastal Reserve WMA, 101
Sawmill Branch Bike/Hike, 102
Schooner Pride, 80
Sea Kayak Carolina, 51
Seabrook Island Equestrian Center, 63
Sewee Shell Mound Interpretive Trail, 98

Sewee Visitor & Environmental Education Center, 103
Simmons Seafood, 131
Smythe Park, 109
Sol Surfers Surf Camp, 59
South Carolina Aquarium, 33, 40
South Tibwin, 99
Splash Island Waterpark, 113, 141
Splash Zone Waterpark, 110, 142
St. Andrew's Park and Playground, 118
Stingrays Hockey, 159
Stono Market and Café, 122
Stono River Stable, 49, 64
Sullivan's Island Park, 117
Sullivan's Trade a Book, 151
Swamp Fox Trailhead, 96-97
The Bicycle Shoppe, 73
The Charleston Museum, 24, 42
The Climbing Wall at James Island County Park, 67, 111
The North Charleston and American Lafrance Fire Museum and Educational Center, 26
The Park, 61
Tiedemann Park Nature Center, 41, 107
Time Out Sport & Ski, 52, 69
Toogoodoo Christmas Tree Farm, 127
Tour Charleston, 29
Truxbury Horse, 99
Twin River Lanes, 154
Wando Shrimp Company, 131
Washo Reserve, 101

Wannamaker County Park, 104,
    116, 142
Waterfront Park, 22, 30, 31, 108
West Ashley Greenway, 92, 93
West Ashley Park, 119
Whirlin' Waters Adventure
Waterpark, 116, 142
White Point Gardens, 94, 108
Whole Foods, 131
Yard Boy Charters, 81